EXCEL 2019

ALL-IN-ONE

Master the new features of
Excel 2019 / Office 365

by
Lokesh Lalwani

MW01015049

FIRST EDITION 2019

Copyright © BPB Publications, India

ISBN: 978-93-88511-582

Distributors:

BPB PUBLICATIONS
20, Ansari Road, Darya Ganj
New Delhi-110002
Ph: 23254990/23254991

DECCAN AGENCIES
4-3-329, Bank Street,
Hyderabad-500195
Ph: 24756967/24756400

MICRO MEDIA
Shop No. 5, Mahendra Chambers,
150 DN Rd. Next to Capital Cinema,
V.T. (C.S.T.) Station, MUMBAI-400 001
Ph: 22078296/22078297

BPB BOOK CENTRE
376 Old Lajpat Rai Market,
Delhi-110006
Ph: 23861747

Published by Manish Jain for BPB Publications, 20 Ansari Road, Darya Ganj, New Delhi-110002 and Printed by him at Repro India Ltd, Mumbai

Dedication

Almighty God, My Family& Friends

About the Author

Lokesh Lalwani is a Microsoft Certified Office Expert with over a decade of experience in the field of training. He is a seasoned entrepreneur and the co-founder of a renowned corporate training firm, Nurture Tech Academy.

He has conducted over a thousand corporate workshops on various topics like advanced Excel, business presentations, Power BI, etc., and has trained over twelve thousand professionals. He has also shared his knowledge on these topics through five pre-recorded courses on world's most popular e-learning platforms, with an average rating of 4.5/5 from over fifteen thousand learners. His motto is, "Life is learning."

Acknowledgements

First and foremost, I would like to thank God for giving me the courage to write this book. I would like to thank everyone at BPB Publications for giving me this opportunity to publish my book.

I would also like to thank my loving and caring mother, Poonam Lalwani, my beautiful wife (my life), Mayanka Lalwani, and my awesome and always supportive brother, Sameer Lalwani, for their endless support and helping me in numerous ways.

Lastly, I would like to thank my critics. Without their criticism, I would have never been able to write this book.

Preface

If you look around in in any organization, be it any department, professionals are using Microsoft Excel. This is the most commonly used spreadsheet program worldwide. It is used by professionals for basic to complex calculations and for data analysis. It is also by far the best for data visualization when compared with other spreadsheet programs. Excel helps businesses clean their raw data and analyze it using some great tools. With the help of Macros, one can even record repetitive tasks, which saves a lot of time on daily basis.

Chapter 1 What's New in Excel 2019/Office 365. It introduces to the new features, functions, charts & graphs, which has been introduced in Excel 2019/Office 365.

Chapter 2 Entering Data in Excel. It describes the ways to enter data into Excel spreadsheets. This can be either typing it manually or importing it from other sources.

Chapter 3 Transforming and Managing Data. This focus on the techniques to transform the raw data and how to manage it. Protection of worksheets/workbooks will also be discussed in this chapter.

Chapter 4 Formulas and Functions. This has the detailed discussion on formula writing and various categories of formulas and functions available in Excel.

Chapter 5 Data Analysis. It describes the most powerful tools to analyze data quickly and effectively. Tools like Pivot Table, Power Pivot, Power Query, Forecast sheet etc.

Chapter 6 Data Visualization. It introduces you to the world of data visualization tools like charts, graphs, Slicers, sparkline, timeline, conditional formatting, Power View etc.

Chapter 7 Data Extraction. It explains data extractions methods from Excel spreadsheets.

Chapter 8 Automation In Excel through Macros. It describes Macros, a tool through which one can record our repetitive actions and run them when needed, to save time and efforts.

Downloading the code bundle and colored images:

Please follow the link to download the
Code Bundle and the *Colored Images* of the book:

https://rebrand.ly/ffdbc

Errata

We take immense pride in our work at BPB Publications and follow best practices to ensure the accuracy of our content to provide with an indulging reading experience to our subscribers. Our readers are our mirrors, and we use their inputs to reflect and improve upon human errors if any, occurred during the publishing processes involved. To let us maintain the quality and help us reach out to any readers who might be having difficulties due to any unforeseen errors, please write to us at :

errata@bpbonline.com

Your support, suggestions and feedbacks are highly appreciated by the BPB Publications' Family.

Table of Contents

CHAPTER 1

What's New in Excel 2019/Office 365

Excel is, by far, the most preferred spreadsheet program in the world. People love it because of its simplicity and easy user interface. The primary focus of Excel is to perform basic to advanced level numeric calculations. Every industry, department, and role is dependent on Excel to perform day-to-day duties as well as data analysis and visualization. Microsoft Excel is available in both offline (Excel 2019) and online (Office 365) versions.

Structure:

In this chapter, we will cover the following topics:

- Why use Excel

- New interface of Excel 2019/Office 365

- Worksheets and workbooks

- New functions in Excel 2019/Office 365

- Easier sharing in Excel 2019/Office 365

- New features in Excel 2019/Office 365

- Enhancements in pivot table

- Publish reports to Power BI

Objective:

The sole objective of this chapter is to familiarize you with the new features and interface of Excel 2019/Office 365. After going through this chapter, you will be able to work around in the new interface of Excel. If you are new to Excel, then this chapter will give you a thorough understanding on how to use worksheets and workbooks. You will also get familiar with the new function introduced in Excel 2019/Office 365. In addition, you will get a hold on the new features. Excel is famous for its amazing feature pivot table, and recently this feature has undergone some updation. Here you will get to dive into them too. You will also learn how to publish excel reports to Power BI.

Why use Excel

Excel can be used for following purposes:

- **Data entering/capturing**: In Excel, data can be entered manually or captured into using Get Data group. In Excel 2019/Office 365, data can be captured from many sources like another file (for example. another Excel workbook, Text/CSV, XML, JSON, Folder, and so on), database (for example. SQL Server, Microsoft Access, Analysis Services, SQL Server Analysis Services), online services (for example Facebook), other sources (from example Table/Range, Web, Microsoft Query, OData Feed, ODBC, OLEDB, Blank Query) or by combining Queries (Merge Query, Append Query).

- **Data cleaning**: Sometimes capturing the data from a non Microsoft application may corrupt the data which needs to be clean first before any analysis can be done on the same. For this Excel provides some very strong and easy to use data cleaning options such as Text to Columns, case change (for example, UPPER, LOWER, PROPER), data extraction from cells (LEFT, RIGHT, MID, FIND, SEARCH), data concatenation (CONCATENATE, &, TextJoin).

- **Data Management**: Although it is important to understand that Excel is not a **Database Management System** (**DBMS**) like Microsoft Access, it still gives us many data management tools like Lookup functionality (VLOOKUP, HLOOKUP, LOOKUP, INDEX, and MATCH, and so on), Sort & Filter, Advanced Filter, Date & Time functions, conditional calculations, financial functions, Statistical functions, and so on.

- **Data analysis**: Microsoft Excel provides a variety of options for analyzing data. Few of the most commonly used options are pivot table and/or Power Pivot, Analysis tool pack, and What-If Analysis.

- **Data visualization**: Microsoft Excel improved its data visualization immensely in Excel 2019/Office 365. The bucket of charts has some new ones in this latest version like Map and Funnel Charts, apart from

Waterfall, Histogram, Sunburst, and TreeMap, which got introduced in the earlier version. Sparkline, Slicer, Timeline, PivotChart and conditional formatting are also a part of data visualization.

- **Data extraction**: Data can be extracted directly on a paper using print command or in soft from as an Excel Workbook, PDF, Microsoft Word, CSV, XML, Web Page, Text, Add-In or XPS, or uploaded to Power BI for further analysis and visualization.

- **Automation**: Almost every Excel user perform some repetitive tasks daily, weekly, bi-weekly, monthly, quarterly, half-early, or yearly. Sensing the need to have some automation solution Microsoft introduced the concept of Macros, where tasks that need to be done more than once can be recorded and let Excel do the same next time.

New interface of Excel 2019/Office 365

The following *Figure 1.1* is a screenshot of Microsoft Excel 2019/Office 365 interface:

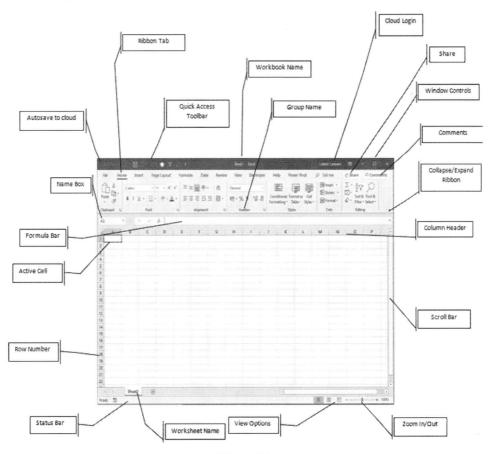

Figure 1.1

Parts of Excel Interface:

- **Autosave to cloud**: While using Office 365, being logged in to Microsoft account will autosave the workbook and any changes made to it. Fear of losing data will be eliminated with this autosave option.

- **Name Box**: This box always shows the active cell address. Any name can be assigned to a cell or a range and can be used in the reference of the same.

- **Formula Bar**: It shows the content of the active cell. It may contain a formula/function, text, or a number that can directly be edited here.

- **Active Cell**: A cell is formed from the intersection of a row and column. By default Excel shows all the cells in gridlines. A green color border on a cell shows that it is active.

- **Row Number**: There are over one million rows and each row are assigned a number.

- **Column Header**: Excel has over sixteen thousand columns in each worksheet. Each column is assigned an alphabet. This can also be changed to numbers through the File tab but the alphabets is a favorite among Excel users.

- **Status Bar**: This shows the current status of Excel. Also, by default, it shows the basic calculation of the selected range of cells.

- **Worksheet Name**: This states the name of the worksheet. Defaults name are sheet1, sheet2, sheet3, and so on. which can be renamed by right clicking on the Worksheet Name | Rename.

- **View Options**: An Excel Worksheet has few view options which can be accessed from here, such as Normal, Page Layout, and Page Break Preview.

- **Zoom In/Out**: Zooming in and out of the worksheet can be accessed from the View tab or can be quickly accessed from here.

- **Scroll Bar**: The size of the scroll bar decreases with an increase in the data in the worksheet. Page down (*Pgdn*) or Page up (*Pgup*) keys can be used as shortcuts to scroll up and down a page at a time.

- **Collapse/Expand Ribbon**: This can be used to pin up the expansion of the ribbon. It is quite handy to have an expanded ribbon.

- **Comments**: This is an Office 365 feature where comments can be added to an Excel file (unlike to a cell).

- **Window Controls**: Excel window can be minimized, resized or closed using the options in this set of controls.

- **Share**: Multiple users can edit the same workbook/worksheet at a time using this feature. Their names can also be seen along the cursors in the sheet.

- **Cloud Login**: Logging in will enable several features like Autosave, Share, Comments, and so on.

- **Workbook Name**: This feature displays the name of the workbook.

- **Quick Access Toolbar (QAT)**: This toolbar is very handy as here one can place their regularly used features of Excel. One can use the same through the *Alt* key and add any function/feature of Excel using a little dropdown in QAT.

- **Ribbon Tab**: By default, Excel provides a set of tabs, and if needed, these can be customized by right clicking on the tab name.

- **Group Name**: Each tab in the ribbon has a certain group that in turn contains a set of options.

Workbooks and Worksheets

An Excel workbook is just a notebook, while an Excel worksheet is like the sheets in that notebook. We can have any number of workbooks we need, and keep them all open simultaneously. A workbook contains worksheets, chart sheets, and macro sheets. We can have unlimited number of sheets in a workbook. By default, the file extension of an Excel workbook is .xlsx. An excel workbook can be saved in several file formats (shown in *Figure 1.2*):

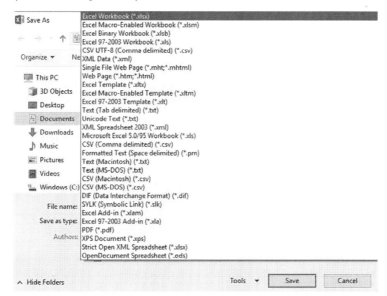

Figure 1.2

We can also rename the workbook at the time of saving it (as shown in *Figure 1.3*):

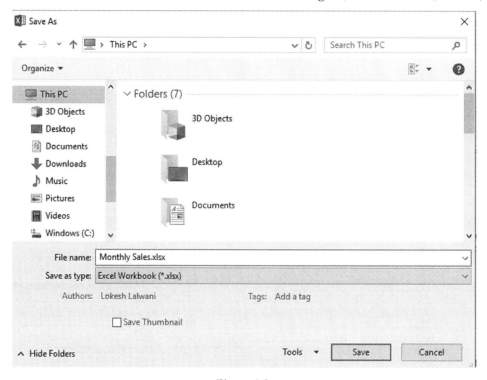

Figure 1.3

A blank workbook is shown in the following screenshot:

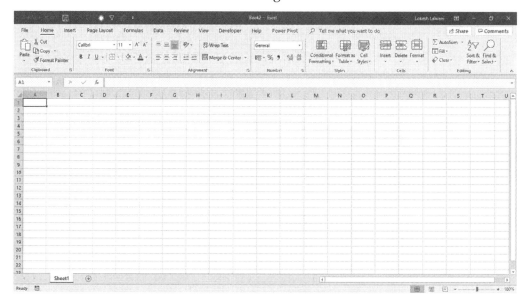

Figure 1.4

A worksheet is a combination of columns and rows and the intersection of the same is called **cell**. A worksheet has over a million rows and over sixteen thousand columns, giving us billions of cells. The moment you delete columns, rows, or cells, Excel will insert those many fresh columns, rows, or cells, thus maintaining their default number.

A worksheet can be renamed by double or right clicking and typing in the new name (see *Figure 1.5*):

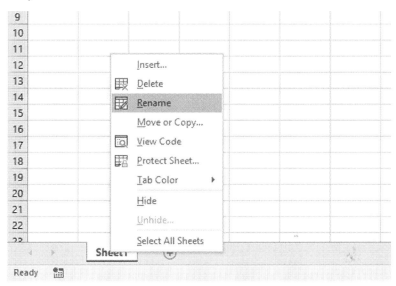

Figure 1.5

Clicking on the + (plus) sign will insert a new worksheet (see *Figure 1.6*). Or you can go to Home tab | select Insert | and then select Insert Worksheet:

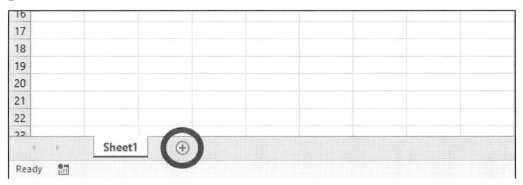

Figure 1.6

A sheet can be deleted by right-clicking on the sheet name. Move or Copy is an amazing option for any Excel user when it comes to applying similar formatting changes to a cell with fresh data. This option can also be used by right-clicking on the sheet name (see *Figure 1.7*):

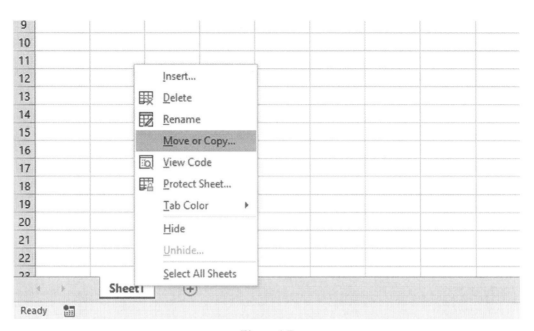

Figure 1.7

New Functions in Excel 2019/Office 365

Excel 2019/Office 365 has several new long-awaited functions in the fields of text and conditional calculations. Exciting, right? So without further ado, let's take a look at the list of all the new functions.

Exercise file

A workbook containing the exercise files used in this chapter for all the new functions, is available on https://rebrand.ly/ffdbc, the file is named **1.1 New Functions.xlsx**. You can download it and practice along.

CONCAT

Unlike CONCATENATE function, CONCAT has the capability to join multiple cells at one go, in other words, instead of referring to single cells, you can give a range of cells and the content of all the cells within that range will be moved to one cell. This function has replaced CONCATENATE, but it is still available for compatibility with previous versions.

Syntax:

```
CONCAT(text1, [text2],….)
```

- **text1 (required)**: It could be text, a cell, or even a range of cells.
- **text2 (optional)**: Additional text that needs to be joined with text1. This could be text, a cell, or even a range of cells.

Example:

Let's take an example of customer data where the customer address is mentioned in multiple columns, and that needs to be concatenated so that a single address line can be printed on a letter to be mailed to the customer. Let's open the function (see *Figure 1.8*):

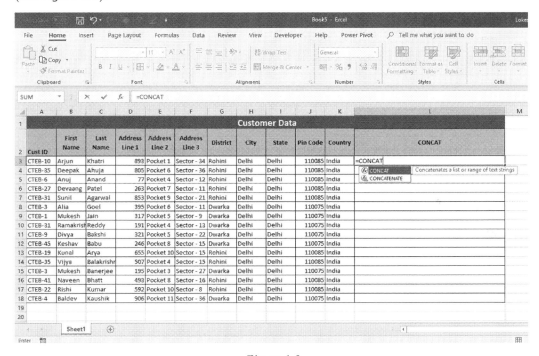

Figure 1.8

As you can see in *Figure 1.8*, CONCATENATE function still exists. However, we have used CONCAT, where we have selected the complete range of address lines, that is, from column D to column K, and typed it as a range in CONCAT. As a result, the columns got joined in a single cell (see *Figure 1.9* and *Figure 1.10*). Practice file available in folder Module 1 | 1. New Functions:

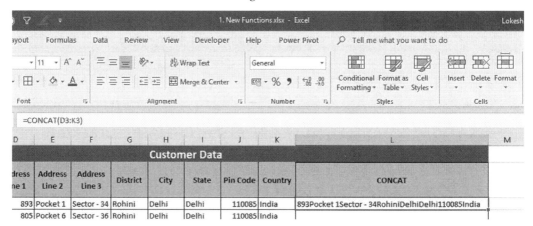

Figure 1.9

Figure 1.10

TEXTJOIN

This is an advanced CONCAT function that can join text from multiple cells and even it can accept a delimiter. In the previous example, we used CONCAT to join different address line items but it was without a separator (delimiter). TEXTJOIN gives us the option to set a delimiter when concatenating text from different cells.

Syntax:

```
TEXTJOIN(delimiter, ignore_empty, text1, [text2], …)
```

- delimiter: This is the required term. It is a common character(s) that needs to be added after each cell/text in the range.

- ignore_empty: This is the required term. This will ignore all the empty cells in the selected range.

- text1: This is the required term. This could be text, a cell, a range, or a range of cells

- text2: This is optional. This is the next cell, text, or range that needs to be joined with **text1** argument.

Example:

Let's take the same data that we used in the example for CONCAT function (that is, *Figure 1.8*). Here, we have used TEXTJOIN function along with "," (comma followed by space) as a delimiter. Ignoring any blank cells, a range of cells is selected (see *Figure 1.11*):

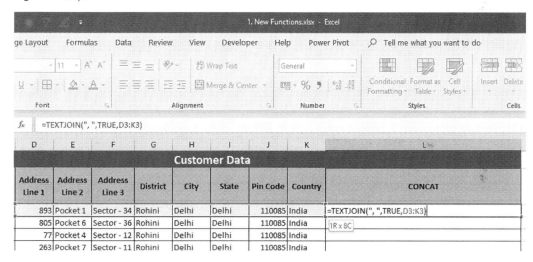

Figure 1.11

The result of TEXTJOIN function will as follows:

```
893, Pocket 1, Sector - 34, Rohini, Delhi, Delhi, 110085, India
```

SWITCH

It evaluates an expression against a list of values and gives result corresponding to the first match in the data. In other words, SWITCH function will match all the values in its Value arguments with the expression argument and return the result accordingly.

Syntax:

```
=SWITCH(expression, Value1, result1, [Value2, result2]…)
```

- Expression: This is a required argument. It can be a constant, a cell reference or reference to a cell having formula that will return a value.

- Value1: This is a required argument. It's a value that needs to be matched with the expression.

- result1: This is the required argument. If Value1 matches with the expression then this function will return the value placed in this argument.

- Value2: This is an optional argument. If there is more than one value to be matched with the expression, then it can be entered in Value2, Value3, and so on.

- result2: This is an optional argument. If more than one value needs to be matched with the expression, then the subsequent results needs to be entered in these arguments.

Example:

The following table shows a list of months and the respective monthly expenses. On the right-hand side, March and July months are listed to match with the Monthly Expenses table and enter the expenses under the Total Expenses column. So, let's use the SWITCH function in column F, that is, Total Expenses, to obtain the value from column B. See *Figure 1.12*:

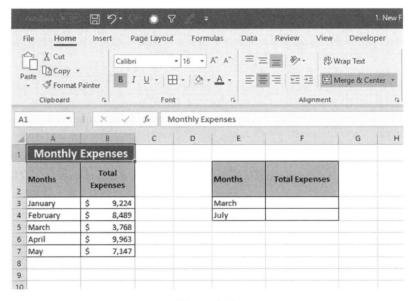

Figure 1.12

The data obtained using SWITCH function is shown in the following *Figure 1.13*:

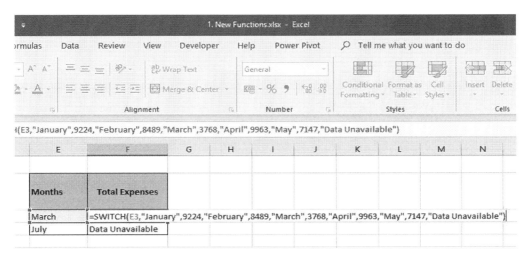

Figure 1.13

Here, the result for this function for March is 3768. But for July it is Data Unavailable because the month of July is not mentioned in this function and so it will assign it the last argument, that is, Data Unavailable. See the following *Figure 1.14*:

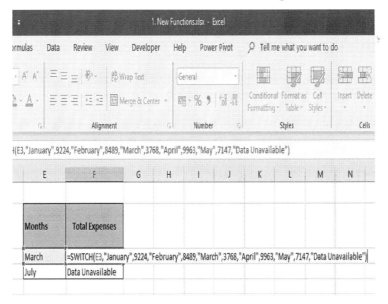

Figure 1.14

MAXIFS

It returns the maximum value out of a range on the basis of one or more criteria.

Syntax:

=MAXIFS (max_range, range1, criteria1, [range2], [criteria2], ...)

- max_range: This is a required argument. This is a range of cells from which one needs to find the maximum value.

- range1: This is a required argument. This is the range for the first criterion range

- criteria1: This is the required argument. The first criterion needs to match in range1.

- range2: This is an optional argument for subsequent criteria range.

- criteria2: This is an optional argument for subsequent criteria that will fall in range2.

Example:

In the following *Figure 1.15*, shows a list of all the employees of a company. Their designations and salaries are mentioned. On the right-hand side, we need to find the maximum Salary of only Sr. Exe designation:

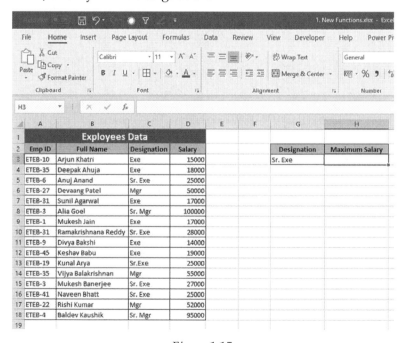

Figure 1.15

If we use the MAX function here, it will return the maximum possible value from the complete range, ignoring the designation. So, here we can use MAXIFS to get the maximum value from the Salary column for the Sr. Exe designation. See the following *Figure 1.16*:

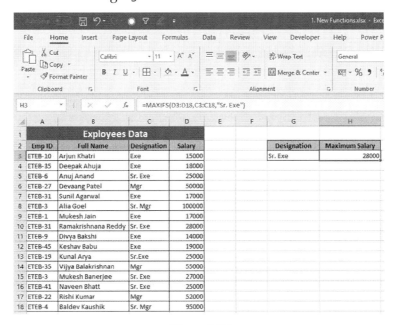

Figure 1.16

Ultimately it will fetch the maximum salary being paid to any Sr. Exe in the company as $28,000. See the following *Figure 1.17*:

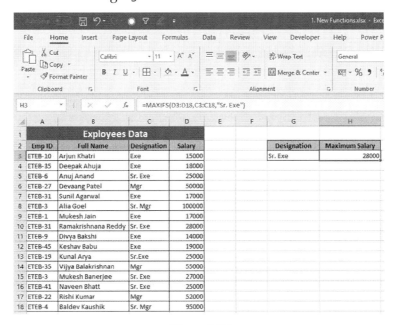

Figure 1.17

MINIFS

It returns the minimum value from a range on the basis of one or more criteria.

Syntax:

`=MINIFS (min_range, range1, criteria1, [range2], [criteria2], ...)`

- min_range: This is a required argument. This is a range of cells from which one needs to find the minimum value.

- range1: This is a required argument. This is the range for the first criterion.

- criteria1: This is a required argument. The first criterion needs to match in range1.

- range2: This is an optional argument for subsequent criteria range.

- criteria2: This is an optional argument for subsequent criteria that will fall in range2.

Example:

In the following *Figure 1.18*, shows a list of all the employees of a company. Their designations and salaries are mentioned. On the right-hand side, we need to find the minimum Salary of only Exe designation:

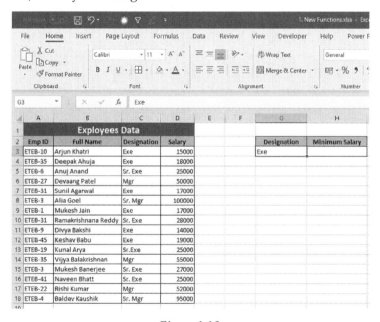

Figure 1.18

If we use the MIN function here, it will return the minimum possible value from the complete range, ignoring the designation. So, here we can use MINIFS to get the minimum value from the Salary column for the Exe designation. See the following *Figure 1.19*:

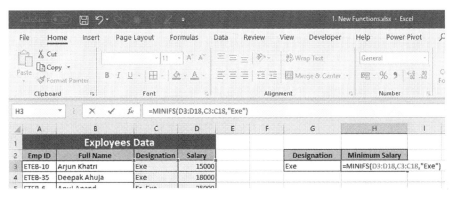

Figure 1.19

Ultimately it will fetch the minimum salary being paid to any Exe in the company as $14,000. See *Figure 1.20*:

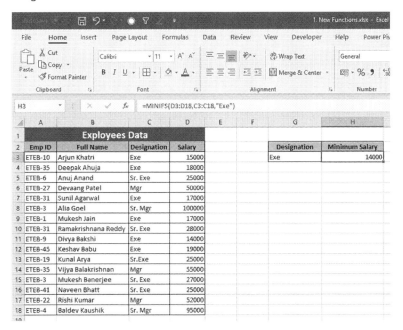

Figure 1.20

IFS

It is a replacement for Nested IF, which is very popular among users of older version of Excel. The IFS function helps in evaluating multiple conditions without the need for the Nested IF function. IFS is much easier to write and read.

Syntax:

```
=IFS (logical_test1, value_if_true1,[logical_test2, value_if_true2]…)
```

Arguments:

- logical_test1: It is the required argument. It is the first condition/ criterion that needs to be judged.

- value_if_true1: This is a required argument. It's the value that the IFS function will return if logical text1 is true.

- logical_test2: This is an optional argument. If logical_test1 is false then the IFS function will jump onto this argument that will check the condition as per this argument.

- value_if_true2: This is an optional argument. This value will be shown if logical_test2 is true else the function will jump to the next argument.

Example:

Here we have a list of employees and their performance scores are mentioned. We need to assign grades to them on the basis of their scores as per the grades table given on the right side. See the following *Figure 1.21*:

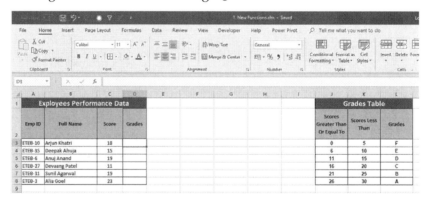

Figure 1.21

The IFS function will be applied in column D to get the grades. See the following *Figure 1.22*:

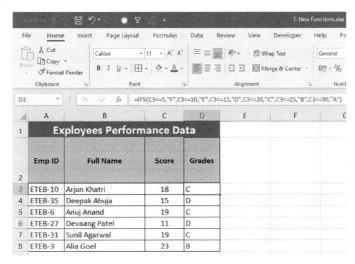

```
=IFS(C3<=5,"F",C3<=10,"E",C3<=15,"D",C3<=20,"C",C3<=25,"B",C3<=30,"A")
```

After applying the preceding function, we will obtain the following results. See the following *Figure 1.23*:

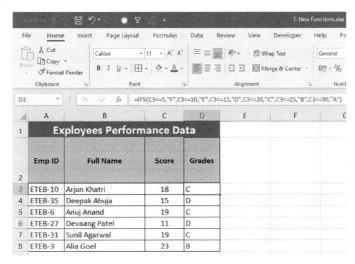

Figure 1.23

New charts in Excel 2019/Office 365

Two new charts have been introduced in the latest version of Excel. Let's discuss the same in detail.

Exercise file

A workbook containing the exercise files used in this chapter for new charts, is available on https://rebrand.ly/ffdbc, The file is named 1.2 New Charts.xlsx. You can download it and practice along.

Map charts

It is a type of chart that shows categories across geographical regions. It uses Microsoft Bing search engine to fetch the visual presentation of each respective data point on the chart.

Example:

Let's take an example of Indian population by state and plot it on a map. The data for the same can be found in practice file named New Charts.xlsx.

The data looks as shown in the following *Figure 1.24*:

Figure 1.24

Select the Data | Insert | Map and then select the predefined map. This will create an Indian geographical region. See *Figure 1.25*:

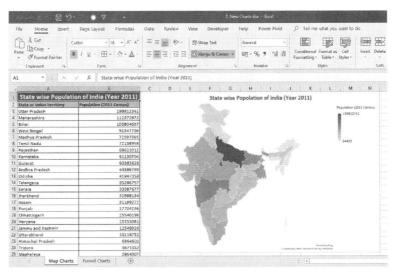

Figure 1.25

Formatting options are discussed in detail under *Charts lecture* **later in this book.**

Funnel chart

It shows values across multiple categories and displays them in the shape of a funnel (in descending order).

Example:

Figure 1.26 below shows customers who use their mobile company's application to pay bills; the customers are categorized by age group:

	A	B
1	**# of Customers paying bills using Mobile application**	
2	**Age Group (years)**	**# of Customers**
3	21 to 30	8,489
4	31 to 40	5,768
5	41 to 50	2,963
6	>50	747

Figure 1.26

To create a Funnel chart, go to the Insert | Charts Group | Insert Funnel | Select the Funnel chart.

See the following *Figure 1.27*:

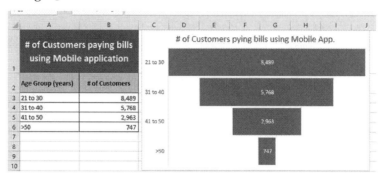

Figure 1.27

Easier sharing in Excel 2019/Office 365

Insert recent links

With this option, it becomes much easier to insert a hyperlink to any of your files that are saved on the cloud; other files can also be linked here using insert the Link option.

Following are the steps to insert a link:

1. Place the cursor at the position where you need to insert the link.

2. Go to Insert | Click on the dropdown of the Link option.

3. It will show all the recently used files that are on the cloud. Select the one you want and click ok. See the following *Figure 1.28* (image source: Office.com):

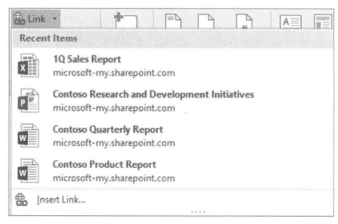

Figure 1.28

Or

If there are no files saved on the cloud, then Insert Link... option can also be used. See the following *Figure 1.29*:

Figure 1.29

View and store previous versions of Workbook

Office 365 continuously saves the previous versions of the workbook, along with version history, so that one can access it if required and restore the same.

To access the same:

1. Click on File tab

4. Click on Info section

5. Click on Version History

Swiftly store workbook in recently used folders

Clicking on Save as and browsing through the folders is a thing of the past. This latest version of MS Office shows us the list of all the recently used folders and helps us quickly save the file in any folder without exiting MS Excel. Click on the File | Save As | and then select Recent. See the following *Figure 1.30*:

Figure 1.30

New features in Excel 2019/Office 365

Accuracy in selection of cells and ranges

Often when choosing different cells or ranges in Excel, you inadvertently select unwanted/unnecessary ones. Now with the Deselect tool, you can deselect any cells inside the selected range. Pressing the *Ctrl* key, you can click or click and drag to deselect any cells or ranges inside a selection. On the off chance that you have to reselect any of those cells or ranges, keep holding the *Ctrl* key and reselect those cells (for Mac, use the *Cmd* key). See the following *Figure 1.31*:

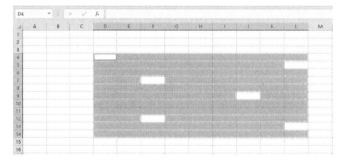

Figure 1.31

Adding superscript and subscript to QAT

Now you can add superscripts and subscripts to the **Quick Access Toolbar** (**QAT**). Then the same can be accessed using a hot key or by clicking on the same. Steps to add superscripts and subscripts in QAT are as follows:

1. Click on **Quick Access Toolbar**. See the following *Figure 1.32*:

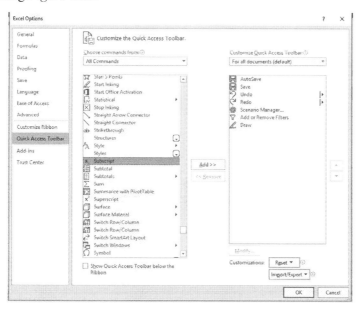

Figure 1.32

6. Under **Popular Commands**, select **Subscript** and **Superscript** one by one. See the following *Figure 1.33*:

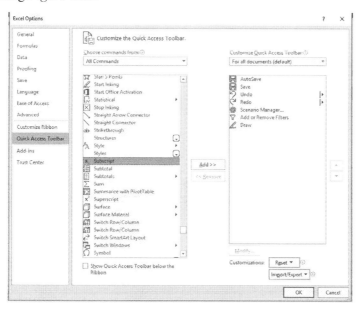

Figure 1.33

7. Click **OK** and the superscripts/subscripts will become a part of your QAT. Now you can access them by pressing the *Alt* key also. See the following *Figure 1.34*:

Figure 1.34

Enhanced autocomplete

Gone are the days when you had to spell out the complete function name correctly. Excel has improved it's autocomplete formula feature so much that now you have to just type any part of the function and it will suggest you any function that has those keywords. For instance, suppose you need to use the NETWORKDAYS function, but you can't recollect how it is spelled. If you simply type =DAYS, the autocomplete menu will display all the functions that contain DAYS, including, NETWORKDAYS.

New office themes

Presently there are four office themes that you can choose from: Colorful, Dark Gray, Black and White.

Under the File tab, choose Options, General, Personalize your copy of Microsoft Office, and then select Office Theme | Choose Theme | OK and enjoy the new look.

See the following *Figure 1.35*:

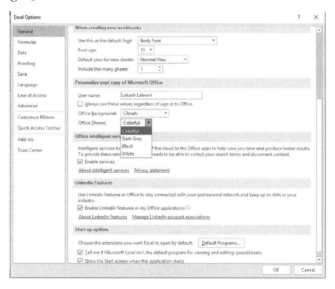

Figure 1.35

Ease of using Microsoft translator

Select the cell that has the word or sentence to be translated or just write the same in the inbuilt Microsoft Translator and done!

Click on the Review tab, and then select Translate. Then either select the cell or just type in the Translator pane on the right-hand side. See the following *Figure 1.36*:

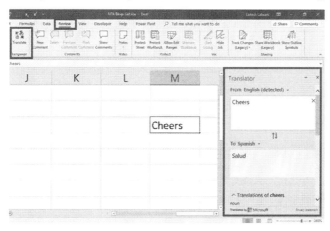

Figure 1.36

No annoying warnings when saving CSV files

In Excel 2019/Office 365, there will be no warnings when you save any CSV file.

Now CSV (UTF-8) also supported

Now you can save an Excel file into CSV (UTF-8) (comma delimited) format. This supports a greater number of characters than the CSV file format. Excel also gives better support to non-english characters.

Data Loss Protection (DLP) in Excel

Excel is now equipped with real-time data scan based on a set of predefined policies of most common sensitive data such as social security number, and CC number. This feature is also synchronized with other Office applications and helps organizations secure such data stored in Exchange, SharePoint, and OneDrive.

Enhancements in pivot table

Really useful improvements can be found in Excel 2019/Office 365. They are explained as follows.

Personalized pivot table

In earlier versions, customizations to the pivot table layout were temporary and were limited to the current table only, but now we can set the layout in advance for any future tables.

To set the default layout, select the File tab, Options, Data, and then click on Edit Default Layout... (see the following *Figure 1.37*):

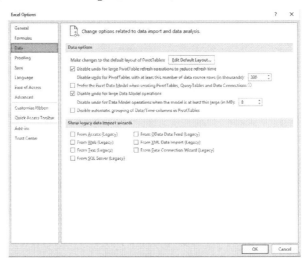

Figure 1.37

You can adjust almost all the parts of a table. Layout of an existing table can also be added as a default layout by just selecting a cell from within the table. See the following *Figure 1.38*:

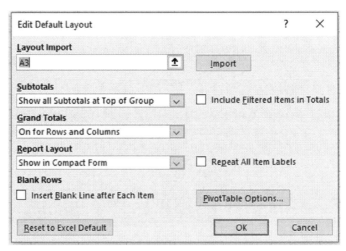

Figure 1.38

Field search enabled

The Search option is now available for the file you are looking for in a field list. See the following *Figure 1.39*:

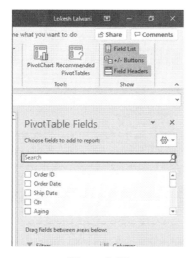

Figure 1.39

Auto relationship detection

The new pivot table can now automatically detect the relationship between the tables you add to the data model.

Drill Down buttons in Pivot Chart

You can now easily drill down the chart to any level of the data. See the following *Figure 1.40*:

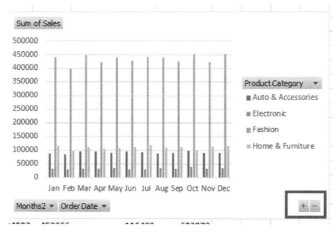

Figure 1.40

Auto date/time grouping

Once you select any date/time field and drop it into any column, or row labels, the pivot table will automatically group them. This grouping can be edited or removed by right clicking on the Field | Group/Ungroup.

Multi-select option (Slicer)

In earlier versions, the *Ctrl* key was needed to select multiple items in a slicer but now a multi select option is part of the header area of any slicer. See the following *Figure 1.41*:

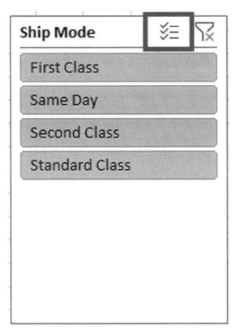

Figure 1.41

Publish to Power BI

This updated feature can be used if you have Power BI subscription. Here, local files can directly be uploaded to Power Bi. Select the File tab, then Publish, and then click on Publish to Power BI. The same can be viewed in a web browser using the Go to Power BI option. See the following *Figure 1.42*:

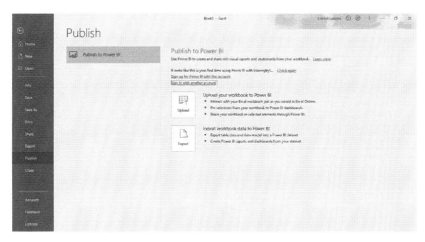

Figure 1.42

Summary

In this chapter, we have discussed the new interface of Excel 2019/Office 365 and how to play around with Excel worksheets and workbooks. We have also got a hold on the new functions introduced in Excel, such as new sharing options and updated general features. Further, we have reviewed the latest updation in pivot table. Excel has also introduced a new feature, under which we can publish reports to Power BI, where further highly interactive dashboards can be prepared.

In the next chapter, we will discuss how to enter data into Excel. There are several ways to enter data into Excel worksheets. You will learn how to enter it manually or through data form (where one transaction can be entered at one time). We will also throw some light on how to import data into Excel from other Excel files, databases, online services, or other sources. In addition, we will discuss how to apply data validation rules to obtain streamlined data.

CHAPTER 2

Entering Data in Excel

Excel is all about data capturing, data transformation, data analysis and data visualization. In this chapter, we will discuss data capturing. Excel gives us two comprehensive ways to enter data in any Worksheet/Workbook, that is, either by entering the data manually or by extracting from other sources that can either be online or offline, on-premise or off-premise. Let's begin by exploring these ways one by one.

Structure:

In this chapter, we will discuss:

- Entering data manually
- Entering data using data form
- Importing data using Get and Transform
- Applying data validation

Objective:

The core objective of this chapter is to explain how to enter data into Excel sheets. Excel provides us several means to do so. Here, you will learn how to enter data manually either by entering it directly into cells or by using data forms and entering one record at a time. You will also learn how to capture data from different sources. Finally, we will discuss data validation, wherein you will learn how to apply rules on cells to ensure desired data quality.

Entering data manually

This is one of the common ways to enter data in an Excel worksheet/workbook.

Just like in a raw field where one can just go and start sowing seeds to get the crop later, here you can just use your fingers and the keyboard to punch in the data. Entering data into an Excel cell is slightly different from other MS Office applications. When typing something in a cell, pressing the *Enter* key or *Tab* key or clicking away from that cell will only commit the cell with the content that we were typing (unlike MS Word).

The major types of data that can be accepted by an Excel cell can be categorized as follows:

- Numeric data
- Text
- Date & Time
- Formulas or functions

Let's take an example of a data set and start discussing the same having all the preceding mentioned data types and see how Excel reacts to them. Assume we are working in the HR (human resources) department of a company and need to enter data related to each of its employee. First, let's open an Excel workbook. now click on cell A1 and type a suitable title for the data, that is, Employee Data. See the following *Figure 2.1*:

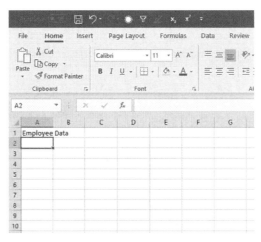

Figure 2.1

As you may have noticed, it seems as if the title Employee Data is taking over B1 cell also. However, that is not the case. As there is nothing in cell B1 and the width of column A is small, Excel is just trying to use the onscreen space to show the complete content in cell A1. But once we enter some data into cell B1, you will see text limited to only cell A1. To solve this problem, you can either expand the width of column A or you can also merge the cells (which we will apply here). Now, we will start entering the column headers for the data that needs to be captured. See the following *Figure 2.2*:

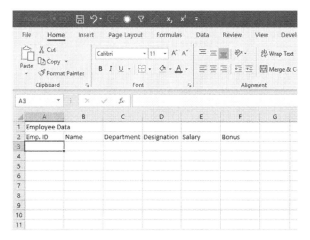

Figure 2.2

After filling in the dummy data, the sheet will look as shown in *Figure 2.3*:

Figure 2.3

Here, the text and numbers are entered in the same manner. Type the formula *=E3*5%* in cell F3 under the Bonus column. Then copy and paste the same formula for all the cells below and bonus will get calculated for all those cells. Merge cells from A1 to F1 by selecting them and then by going to the **Home** tab and selecting **Merge & Center**. Apply a style to the selected range of cells by clicking on the **Home tab** and then Select **Cell Styles**, then **Data and Model** and then **Check Cell**. See the following *Figure 2.4*:

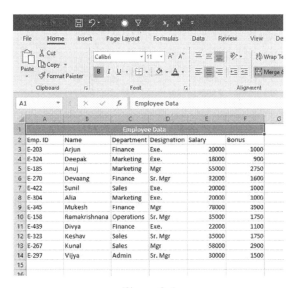

Figure 2.4

Next, apply a style to cells A2 to F2 by clicking on the Home tab and then selecting Cell Styles, then Data and Model and then Output:

Apply cell border to cells A3 to F14 through the Home tab; Font Group, then Bottom Border, and then All Borders. See the following *Figure 2.5*:

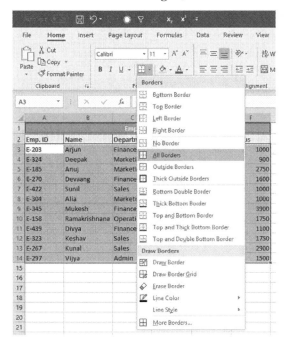

Figure 2.5

Now you will get the employee data in a well-arranged, and formatted manner. See the following *Figure 2.6*:

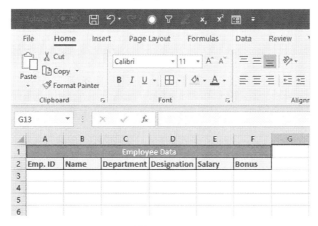

Figure 2.6

Entering data using data form

Another way of entering data in Excel is through data form. A data form is useful when you have multi column data, where we face the common problem of scrolling through each column. Using data forms, you can enter data for up to 32 columns in a single frame without scrolling within the sheet. Let's first enter the headers of the data in a worksheet. (see the following *Figure 2.7*):

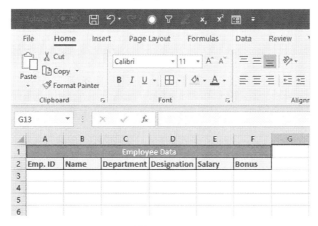

Figure 2.7

First let's add a data form to the **QAT** (**Quick Access Toolbar**):

1. Click on the arrow in QAT.

2. Click on More Commands.

3. In Choose commands from select All Commands.

4. Search for Form... and Click Add >> and then click OK.

Now, select the header row and click on the Form icon in the QAT. Excel will launch the data form and treat the selected row as the header in the form. (see *Figure 2.8*):

Figure 2.8

Now, you can just start entering the data by using the *Tab* key to go to the next cell. After filling in the required data, you can either hit the *Enter* key or click on New button.

Whenever you want to apply a formula to a range of cells, enter the formula in a cell first and then Excel will capture it automatically in the Data Form.

Importing Data using Get & Transform data

Importing data into Excel has never been so comfortable and dynamic. Through this new option of Get & Transform, you can get data from any source that is supported by Excel. Excel opens the Query Editor where the data is transformed, for example, displaying it in a form that can be analyzed without changing the data at the source and then combined with other data sources by creating a data model using the

Relationship Building feature. Lastly, the query can also be saved, shared and in fact used for other workbooks too.

Let's classify the preceding statement into broad steps:

- **Connect**: The first step is to connect with one or multiple data sources. No matter where your organization is maintaining the data, you will find the source here. Microsoft has added several data sources in Excel to connect with. See the following *Figure 2.9*:

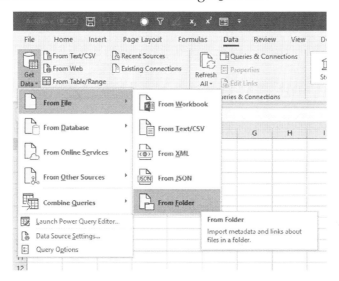

Figure 2.9

You can connect to the following sources:

- From File: Excel Workbook, Text/CSV, XML, JSON or any folder.

- From Database: SQL Server, MS Access, Analysis Services or SQL Server Analysis Services.

- From Online Services: Facebook

- From Other Sources: Table/Range, Web, MS Query, OData Feed, ODBC, OLEDB, or a Blank Query.

- **Transform**: As soon as you connect to a database, Query Editor opens up and records each step, including the one of connecting with the database, so that these recorded steps can help in refreshing the data. At the backend, Query Editor uses **M** language. (See the following *Figure 2.10*):

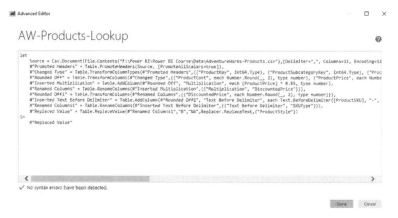

Figure 2.10

In the environment of **Query Editor**, you can transform the data, for example, clean up all the unwanted columns, add calculated columns or Measures using **Data Analysis Expressions** (**DAX**), change data types, merge tables, and so on. Transformation done in the editor will not disturb the data lying at the source. See *Figure 2.11* shows a view of the Query Editor:

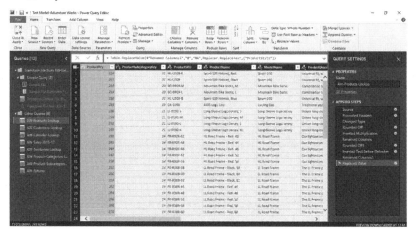

Figure 2.11

- **Combine and share**: After transforming the data, it can be combined with other data sources. A data model can be built from multiple data bases and ultimately a unique view can be generated. Once a query is completed the same can be saved or shared. See the following *Figure 2.12*:

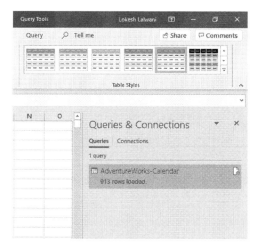

Figure 2.12

Applying data validation

Manual entry usually results in some amount of invalid data. MS Excel offers an amazing tool to restrict the entry of invalid data. For example, if we try to sign up on any online portal by entering an email ID without the @ symbol, the site will not accept it and treat is as invalid. The same functionality is adopted in Data Validation in Excel. Let's understand it with an example. Suppose you would like to capture the employee data of an organization under the fields mentioned in following *Figure 2.13*:

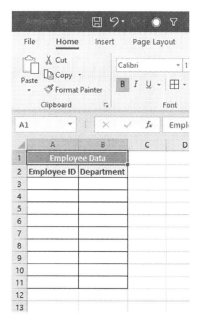

Figure 2.13

Suppose, in the organization, the Employee ID is a 6-character number/code. Therefore, a data validation rule needs to be entered here that will allow only a 6 character Employee ID. Follow the below steps to apply the rule:

1. Select all the cells under Employee ID.

2. Go to the Data tab, select Data Tools Group and then click on Data Validation.

3. Go to the Settings tab and click on Allow and then on Whole number.

4. Set Data as between to100000 to 999999 (See the following *Figure 2.14*):

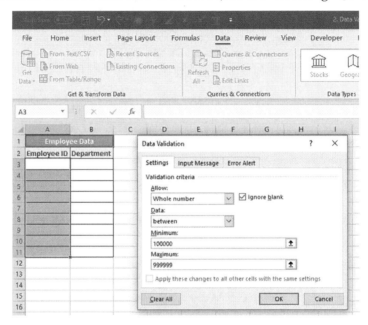

Figure 2.14

5. Input Message, this is optional. (A comment on the data validated cell will show the types of messages that can be accepted into these cells). For example, you can type the message "Please enter a 6 character employee ID". See the following *Figure 2.15*:

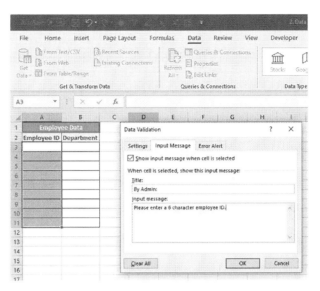

Figure 2.15

6. **Error Alert**: If a user enters data that is not aligned with the data validation rule, then an error message will pop up. Selecting **Stop** under **Style** will allow only those entries that align with the rule, whereas selecting Warning or Information will permit anything beyond the rule too. **Title** and **Error message** are again optional. See the following *Figure 2.16*:

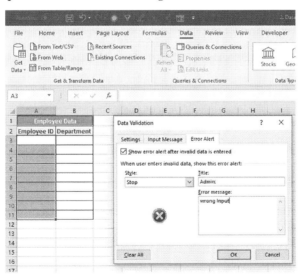

Figure 2.16

7. Click **OK**.

Now, let's test the rule. Type in the number **485** and hit the *Enter* key. You will see an error message. See the following *Figure 2.17*:

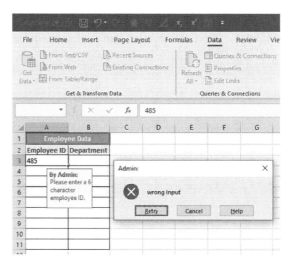

Figure 2.17

Data validation also supports drop-down lists. We can create one for the Department column.

1. Select all the cells under Department.

2. Go to the Data tab, and select Data Tools Group and then Data Validation.

3. Under the Settings tab, go to Allow and then select List.

4. You can either use the elements of the list (if already mentioned in Excel), or you can type them (each element of the list must be separated by a comma). As we don't have a list here, we will type them in. See the following *Figure 2.18*:

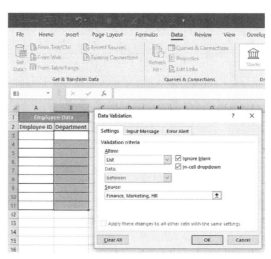

Figure 2.18

As Input Message is optional, we will keep it blank. In the Error Alert, let's go with Warning this time. See the following *Figure 2.19*:

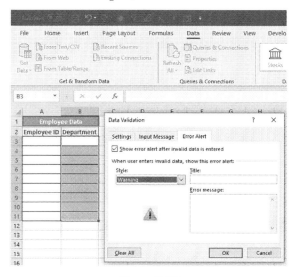

Figure 2.19

This will create a drop-down list as shown in following *Figure 2.20*:

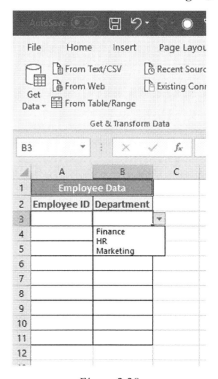

Figure 2.20

You can select an option from the drop-down list. As we have selected Warning as an error alert style, even if we enter something that is not a part of the list, it will get accepted as a temporary entry (but will not become a part of the list) and Excel will show the following message (see the following *Figure 2.21*):

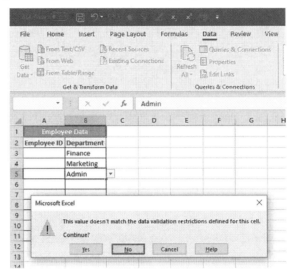

Figure 2.21

Summary

This chapter was all about how to enter data in Excel. We have learnt how to do so manually as well as using data forms. As you have seen, data forms allow one entry at a time, thus facilitating an organized way of data entry. We have also learnt how to capture data from different sources and enter it in Excel. Now, you know how to apply data validation rules on desired cells to restrict data entry.

In the next chapter, we will be discussing how to transform and manage the captured data. Excel has immense capabilities to transform raw data into analysis ready data. Under data transformation, we will learn about sorting, filtering, converting raw data into a table, and finally we will also learn how to protect a worksheet and/or workbook.

CHAPTER 3

Transforming and Managing Data

Once the data is captured, it's now time to transform and, clean it to make it ready for analysis. Thus, transforming and managing the data becomes one of the most important steps here. Excel provides us some beautiful tools such as the Sort feature for arranging the data either in ascending or descending order or in a customized order, or filtering it whenever required. In this chapter, we will discuss such tools which we can use to easily transform and manage the data that we have captured or recorded in Excel so far.

Structure:

In this chapter, we will discuss:

- Sort data on the basis of values, font color, cell color, and so on
- Filter (filter, text filter, custom filter, and advanced filter)
- Converting data into table (understanding multiple table features)
- Protecting workbook and/or worksheet

Objective:

The prime objective of this chapter is to give you overall knowledge on how to transform and manage your captured data. After going through this chapter, you will be able to arrange your data on the basis of its cell value, font color, cell color, and so on. You will also get a hold on the different features of the Filter command, including how to filter your data using Advanced filter. You will also be able to protect your workbook/worksheet before sending it further.

Sort, Filter and Advanced filter

These are the most commonly used features of Excel to get the data into a format where analysis can be done. Sorting helps in arranging the data in the desired order, filter helps in slicing off the unwanted data either based on single or multiple items and even sometimes based on conditions. When it comes to filtering the data based on complex conditions then Advanced Filter is what comes into the picture.

Exercise file

A workbook containing the exercise files used in this chapter for Sort & Filter Data in Excel, is available on https://rebrand.ly/ffdbc, the file is named 3.1 Sort & Filter Data in Excel.xlsx. You can download it and practice along.

Sorting data in Excel

Sorting in Excel is all about arranging data in ascending or descending order, or in a customized order. Sorting can also be done either vertically or horizontally.

Let us take the example of Employee Data of a company and understand sorting function in Excel (see the following *Figure 3.1*):

	A	B	C	D	E	F
1			Employee Data			
2	Emp. ID	Name	Department	Designation	Salary	Bonus
3	E-203	Arjun	Finance	Exe.	20000	1000
4	E-324	Deepak	Marketing	Exe.	18000	900
5	E-185	Anuj	Marketing	Mgr	55000	2750
6	E-270	Devaang	Finance	Sr. Mgr	32000	1600
7	E-422	Sunil	Sales	Exe.	20000	1000
8	E-304	Alia	Marketing	Exe.	20000	1000
9	E-345	Mukesh	Finance	Mgr	78000	3900
10	E-158	Ramakrishnana	Operations	Sr. Mgr	35000	1750
11	E-439	Divya	Finance	Exe.	22000	1100
12	E-323	Keshav	Sales	Sr. Mgr	35000	1750
13	E-267	Kunal	Sales	Mgr	58000	2900
14	E-297	Vijya	Admin	Sr. Mgr	30000	1500
15						

Figure 3.1

Sorting by Number: Let's sort the data for salary in an ascending order using the following steps:

1. Select the complete data including headers.

2. Under the Data tab select Sort. This will open a dialog box for customized sorting (see the following *Figure 3.2*):

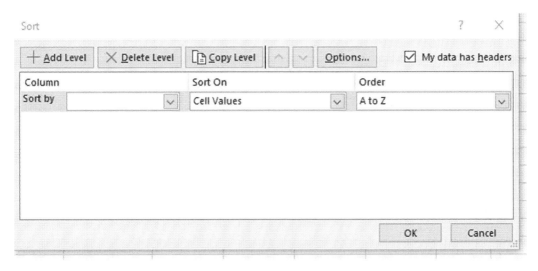

Figure 3.2

3. Choose Salary in Sort by, cell values in Sort On and smallest to largest as the Order.

4. Click Ok.

The data is now sorted as shown in the following *Figure 3.3*):

	A	B	C	D	E	F
1				Employee Data		
2	Emp. ID	Name	Department	Designation	Salary	Bonus
3	E-324	Deepak	Marketing	Exe.	18000	900
4	E-203	Arjun	Finance	Exe.	20000	1000
5	E-422	Sunil	Sales	Exe.	20000	1000
6	E-304	Alia	Marketing	Exe.	20000	1000
7	E-439	Divya	Finance	Exe.	22000	1100
8	E-297	Vijya	Admin	Sr. Mgr	30000	1500
9	E-270	Devaang	Finance	Sr. Mgr	32000	1600
10	E-158	Ramakrishnana	Operations	Sr. Mgr	35000	1750
11	E-323	Keshav	Sales	Sr. Mgr	35000	1750
12	E-185	Anuj	Marketing	Mgr	55000	2750
13	E-267	Kunal	Sales	Mgr	58000	2900
14	E-345	Mukesh	Finance	Mgr	78000	3900
15						

Figure 3.3

Sorting by Text: Data can also be sorted on the basis of text. Let's take the previous example again. Here, we will sort the data by "Department" in Z to A order as follows:

1. Select the complete data including headers.

2. Under the Data tab select Sort. This will open the Sort dialog box again.

3. Choose Department in Sort by, cell values in Sort On and Z to A as the Order.

4. Click Ok.

The data is now sorted as shown in the following *Figure 3.4*):

	A	B	C	D	E	F
1			Employee Data			
2	Emp. ID	Name	Department	Designation	Salary	Bonus
3	E-422	Sunil	Sales	Exe.	20000	1000
4	E-323	Keshav	Sales	Sr. Mgr	35000	1750
5	E-267	Kunal	Sales	Mgr	58000	2900
6	E-158	Ramakrishnana	Operations	Sr. Mgr	35000	1750
7	E-324	Deepak	Marketing	Exe.	18000	900
8	E-304	Alia	Marketing	Exe.	20000	1000
9	E-185	Anuj	Marketing	Mgr	55000	2750
10	E-203	Arjun	Finance	Exe.	20000	1000
11	E-439	Divya	Finance	Exe.	22000	1100
12	E-270	Devaang	Finance	Sr. Mgr	32000	1600
13	E-345	Mukesh	Finance	Mgr	78000	3900
14	E-297	Vijya	Admin	Sr. Mgr	30000	1500

Figure 3.4

Sorting by Cell Color: We can sort data by Cell Color or Font Color. In the following *Figure 3.5*, some of the employee IDs have been highlighted in yellow color.

	A	B	C	D	E	F
1			Employee Data			
2	Emp. ID	Name	Department	Designation	Salary	Bonus
3	E-422	Sunil	Sales	Exe.	20000	1000
4	E-323	Keshav	Sales	Sr. Mgr	35000	1750
5	E-267	Kunal	Sales	Mgr	58000	2900
6	E-158	Ramakrishnana	Operations	Sr. Mgr	35000	1750
7	E-324	Deepak	Marketing	Exe.	18000	900
8	E-304	Alia	Marketing	Exe.	20000	1000
9	E-185	Anuj	Marketing	Mgr	55000	2750
10	E-203	Arjun	Finance	Exe.	20000	1000
11	E-439	Divya	Finance	Exe.	22000	1100
12	E-270	Devaang	Finance	Sr. Mgr	32000	1600
13	E-345	Mukesh	Finance	Mgr	78000	3900
14	E-297	Vijya	Admin	Sr. Mgr	30000	1500

Figure 3.5

We will sort this data in such a way that all the employees with highlighted Emp. ID will come at the top. To do this task, we will follow these steps:

1. Select the complete data including headers.

2. Under the Data tab select Sort. This will open the Sort dialog box.

3. Choose Emp. ID in Sort by, Cell Color in Sort On and the color you want as the Order. See the following *Figure 3.6*:

Figure 3.6

4. Click Ok.

See the following *Figure 3.7*:

	A	B	C	D	E	F
1			Employee Data			
2	Emp. ID	Name	Department	Designation	Salary	Bonus
3	E-267	Kunal	Sales	Mgr	58000	2900
4	E-304	Alia	Marketing	Exe.	20000	1000
5	E-439	Divya	Finance	Exe.	22000	1100
6	E-422	Sunil	Sales	Exe.	20000	1000
7	E-323	Keshav	Sales	Sr. Mgr	35000	1750
8	E-158	Ramakrishnana	Operations	Sr. Mgr	35000	1750
9	E-324	Deepak	Marketing	Exe.	18000	900
10	E-185	Anuj	Marketing	Mgr	55000	2750
11	E-203	Arjun	Finance	Exe.	20000	1000
12	E-270	Devaang	Finance	Sr. Mgr	32000	1600
13	E-345	Mukesh	Finance	Mgr	78000	3900
14	E-297	Vijya	Admin	Sr. Mgr	30000	1500

Figure 3.7

Sorting by Font Color: Sorting can also be done on the basis of Font Color. As shown in the following *Figure 3.8*, some of the numbers under the Bonus column are in red font:

◢	A	B	C	D	E	F
1			Employee Data			
2	Emp. ID	Name	Department	Designation	Salary	Bonus
3	E-267	Kunal	Sales	Mgr	58000	2900
4	E-304	Alia	Marketing	Exe.	20000	1000
5	E-439	Divya	Finance	Exe.	22000	1100
6	E-422	Sunil	Sales	Exe.	20000	1000
7	E-323	Keshav	Sales	Sr. Mgr	35000	1750
8	E-158	Ramakrishnana	Operations	Sr. Mgr	35000	1750
9	E-324	Deepak	Marketing	Exe.	18000	900
10	E-185	Anuj	Marketing	Mgr	55000	2750
11	E-203	Arjun	Finance	Exe.	20000	1000
12	E-270	Devaang	Finance	Sr. Mgr	32000	1600
13	E-345	Mukesh	Finance	Mgr	78000	3900
14	E-297	Vijya	Admin	Sr. Mgr	30000	1500

Figure 3.8

Now follow these steps to sort the employee data such that the numbers in red font appear at the top under the Bonus column:

1. Select the complete data including headers.

2. Under the Data tab select Sort. This will open the Sort dialog box.

3. Choose Bonus in Sort by, Font Color in Sort On and the color you want in Order. See the following *Figure 3.9*:

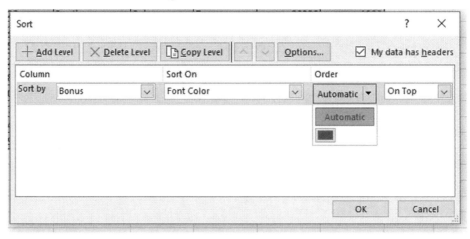

Figure 3.9

4. Click Ok.

See the following *Figure 3.10*:

▲	A	B	C	D	E	F
1			Employee Data			
2	Emp. ID	Name	Department	Designation	Salary	Bonus
3	E-304	Alia	Marketing	Exe.	20000	1000
4	E-422	Sunil	Sales	Exe.	20000	1000
5	E-324	Deepak	Marketing	Exe.	18000	900
6	E-270	Devaang	Finance	Sr. Mgr	32000	1600
7	E-267	Kunal	Sales	Mgr	58000	2900
8	E-439	Divya	Finance	Exe.	22000	1100
9	E-323	Keshav	Sales	Sr. Mgr	35000	1750
10	E-158	Ramakrishnana	Operations	Sr. Mgr	35000	1750
11	E-185	Anuj	Marketing	Mgr	55000	2750
12	E-203	Arjun	Finance	Exe.	20000	1000
13	E-345	Mukesh	Finance	Mgr	78000	3900
14	E-297	Vijya	Admin	Sr. Mgr	30000	1500

Figure 3.10

Multi-Level sorting: So far, we have discussed single level sorting. Using multi-level sorting, employee data in the previous example can be sorted Department wise in an ascending order and at the same time Salary wise in a descending order. Add level feature is also available under the Sort dialog box.

Priority of sorting will be given in the level of orders mentioned in the Sort dialog box. For example, in this case, Department column will be given the first priority as it is set as the first level of sorting.

1. Select the complete data including headers.

2. Under the Data tab select Sort. This will open the Sort dialog box.

3. Choose Department in Sort by, Cell Values in Sort On and A to Z as the Order.

4. Click on Add Level.

5. Choose Bonus in Sort by, Cell Values in Sort On and Largest to Smallest as the order. See the following *Figure 3.11*:

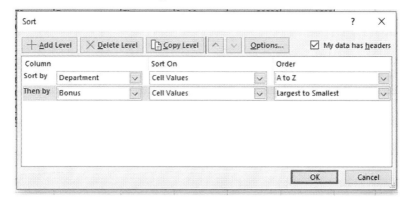

Figure 3.11

6. Click Ok.

See the following *Figure 3.12*:

	A	B	C	D	E	F
1			Employee Data			
2	Emp. ID	Name	Department	Designation	Salary	Bonus
3	E-297	Vijya	Admin	Sr. Mgr	30000	1500
4	E-345	Mukesh	Finance	Mgr	78000	3900
5	E-270	Devaang	Finance	Sr. Mgr	32000	1600
6	E-439	Divya	Finance	Exe.	22000	1100
7	E-203	Arjun	Finance	Exe.	20000	1000
8	E-185	Anuj	Marketing	Mgr	55000	2750
9	E-304	Alia	Marketing	Exe.	20000	1000
10	E-324	Deepak	Marketing	Exe.	18000	900
11	E-158	Ramakrishnana	Operations	Sr. Mgr	35000	1750
12	E-267	Kunal	Sales	Mgr	58000	2900
13	E-323	Keshav	Sales	Sr. Mgr	35000	1750
14	E-422	Sunil	Sales	Exe.	20000	1000

Figure 3.12

In this manner, you can add up to 64 levels. Levels can also be deleted or copied.

Sorting by Custom List: Excel allows customized sorting too. For example, if you want to sort the preceding data by Designation column in such a way that the entries should appear in the order of Exe, then Mgr, and then Sr. Mgr, that is, not in an alphabetical order. So a customized order needs to be created here. Let's take the same example as before and follow the steps to sort the data in a customized order:

1. Select the complete data including headers.

2. Under the Data tab select Sort. This will open the Sort dialog box.

3. Choose Designation in Sort by, Cell Values in Sort On and Custom List… as the Order. See the following *Figure 3.13*:

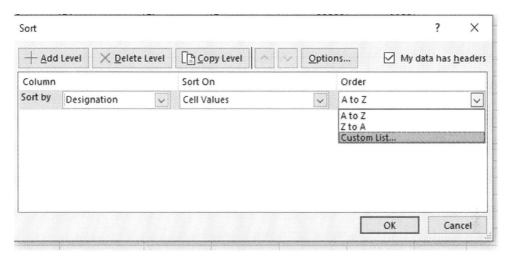

Figure 3.13

The preceding action will immediately trigger another dialog box where you can either choose from the pre-defined custom lists or create your own (see the following *Figure 3.14*):

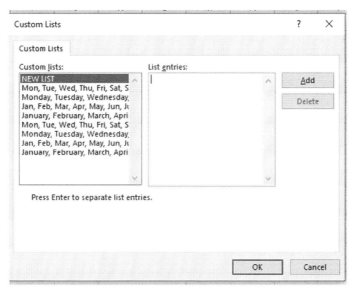

Figure 3.14

As you can see, the pre-defined lists are generic and none of them matches with our current data set. Therefore, we need to create a list from scratch by typing the same under the List entries: box on the right.

See the following *Figure 3.15*:

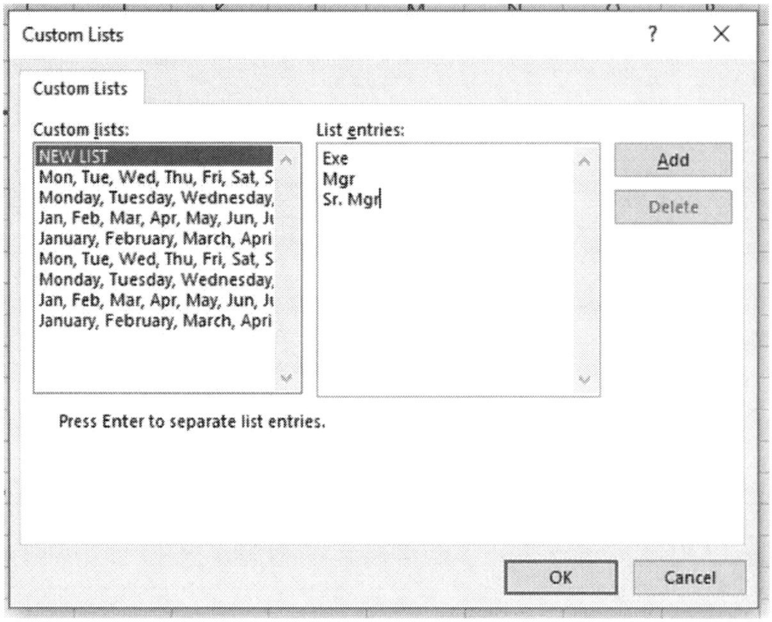

Figure 3.15

4. Click on **Add**, then click **Ok**, and again click **Ok**.

See the following *Figure 3.16*:

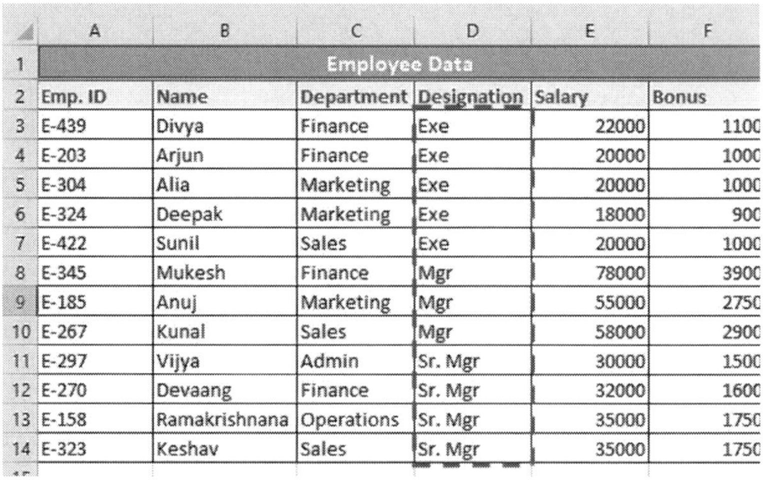

	A	B	C	D	E	F
1			Employee Data			
2	Emp. ID	Name	Department	Designation	Salary	Bonus
3	E-439	Divya	Finance	Exe	22000	1100
4	E-203	Arjun	Finance	Exe	20000	1000
5	E-304	Alia	Marketing	Exe	20000	1000
6	E-324	Deepak	Marketing	Exe	18000	900
7	E-422	Sunil	Sales	Exe	20000	1000
8	E-345	Mukesh	Finance	Mgr	78000	3900
9	E-185	Anuj	Marketing	Mgr	55000	2750
10	E-267	Kunal	Sales	Mgr	58000	2900
11	E-297	Vijya	Admin	Sr. Mgr	30000	1500
12	E-270	Devaang	Finance	Sr. Mgr	32000	1600
13	E-158	Ramakrishnana	Operations	Sr. Mgr	35000	1750
14	E-323	Keshav	Sales	Sr. Mgr	35000	1750

Figure 3.16

Sorting horizontally: So far, we have discussed column wise sorting. The same can be done row-wise also, that is, left to right. Consider the monthly sales of a company as an example. Here the months are listed randomly (not in order). Let's arrange the complete table in such a way that all the columns are arranged in Monthly Sales order. See the following *Figure 3.17*:

I	J	K	L	M	N
Monthly Sales					
March	May	January	June	April	February
110	378	557	215	136	309
828	194	477	646	185	650
799	329	745	475	516	649
818	616	104	136	527	169
207	414	618	467	943	366
358	408	375	640	215	917
264	819	183	114	937	205
866	422	965	834	133	588
644	291	584	970	445	794
882	984	962	738	374	409
435	600	203	288	722	345
730	276	758	588	259	835

Figure 3.17

1. Select the complete data including headers.

2. Under the Data tab select Sort. This will open the Sort dialog box.

3. Click on Sort Options, then select Sort left to right, and then click Ok (see the following *Figure 3.18*):

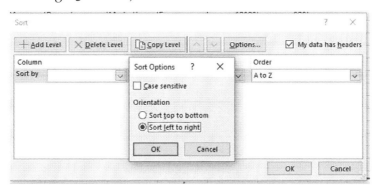

Figure 3.18

4. Select Row 2 (row containing the headers, that is, months) in Sort by, Cell Values in Sort On and Custom Lists as the Order:

5. From Custom Lists, select the one matching our data, that is, the list of all the months written in full (see following *Figure 3.19*):

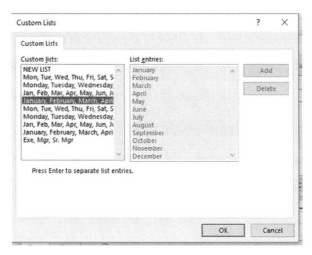

Figure 3.19

1. Click Ok and then again Click Ok. See the following Figure 3.20:

Monthly Sales					
January	February	March	April	May	June
557	309	110	136	378	215
477	650	828	185	194	646
745	649	799	516	329	475
104	169	818	527	616	136
618	366	207	943	414	467
375	917	358	215	408	640
183	205	264	937	819	114
965	588	866	133	422	834
584	794	644	445	291	970
962	409	882	374	984	738
203	345	435	722	600	288
758	835	730	259	276	588

Figure 3.20

Filtering Data in Excel

Data filtering is done when you want to display only those fields from the data that meet a certain condition. Let's consider the example of online shopping. When you wish to buy a pair of shoes from any e-commerce website, you apply filters such as Shoes, Gender, Color, etc. to the product category. Similarly, Excel offers an amazing option to filter data on the basis of criteria such as number, text, cell color, font color, etc. Let's discuss the features in detail.

Number Filter: As Excel is all about playing around with numbers, the Number filter plays a very vital role in transforming and managing data. Let's consider the same example of employee data as in the Sorting section. Now from this list of all the employees, let's list only those employees whose salary is between 30,000 to 60,000.

1. Select the complete data including headers.

2. Under the Data tab select Filter. This will apply a drop-down list on each column header.

3. Click on the drop-down icon in the Salary column. Choose Number filter (Note: This Number filter option is available because Excel has detected out that this active column has numbers) Then choose Between; this will open a dialog box. Type **30000** in front of is greater than or equal to and **60000** in front of is less than or equal to (see the following *Figure 3.21*):

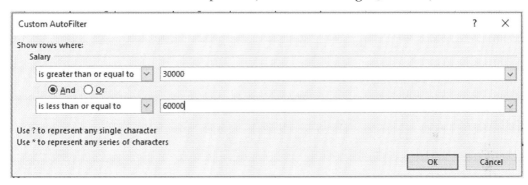

Figure 3.21

4. Click Ok.

This will give you the filtered data (see the following *Figure 3.22*):

	A	B	C	D	E	F
1	Employee Data					
2	Emp. ID ▾	Name ▾	Departme ▾	Designati ▾	Salary ⫴	Bonus ▾
5	E-185	Anuj	Marketing	Mgr	55000	2750
6	E-270	Devaang	Finance	Sr. Mgr	32000	1600
10	E-158	Ramakrish	Operations	Sr. Mgr	35000	1750
12	E-323	Keshav	Sales	Sr. Mgr	35000	1750
13	E-267	Kunal	Sales	Mgr	58000	2900
14	E-297	Vijya	Admin	Sr. Mgr	30000	1500

Figure 3.22

Text Filter: If the data to be filtered is text, then Excel will show us the Text filter option. Now let's list only those employees who are either Mgr or Sr. Mgr.

1. Select the complete data including headers.

2. Under the Data tab select Filter. This will apply a drop-down list on each column header.

3. Click on the drop-down icon in the Department column. Choose Text filter (Note: Text filter option is available because Excel has detected that this active column has text). Then choose contains; this will open a dialog box. Type Mgr (see the following *Figure 3.23*):

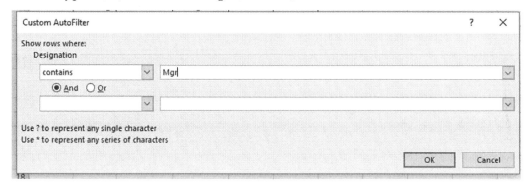

Figure 3.23

4. Click Ok.

You will see the filtered data as shown in the following *Figure 3.24*:

	A	B	C	D	E	F
1	Employee Data					
2	Emp. ID ▾	Name ▾	Departme ▾	Designati ▾	Salary ▾	Bonus ▾
5	E-185	Anuj	Marketing	Mgr	55000	2750
6	E-270	Devaang	Finance	Sr. Mgr	32000	1600
9	E-345	Mukesh	Finance	Mgr	78000	3900
10	E-158	Ramakrish	Operations	Sr. Mgr	35000	1750
12	E-323	Keshav	Sales	Sr. Mgr	35000	1750
13	E-267	Kunal	Sales	Mgr	58000	2900
14	E-297	Vijya	Admin	Sr. Mgr	30000	1500

Figure 3.24

Cell Color Filter: Data can also be filtered on the basis of cell color. Sometimes we use colors to mark cells for later reference. Now instead of going through the entire data set looking for the colored cells, you can use the Cell Color filter to display only those cells. In *Figure 3.25* below, some of the cells containing employee IDs have been filled with yellow color. Let's see how to filter and display only those employees whose employee IDs are colored.

	A	B	C	D	E	F
1			Employee Data			
2	Emp. ID	Name	Department	Designation	Salary	Bonus
3	E-203	Arjun	Finance	Exe.	20000	1000
4	E-324	Deepak	Marketing	Exe.	18000	900
5	E-185	Anuj	Marketing	Mgr	55000	2750
6	E-270	Devaang	Finance	Sr. Mgr	32000	1600
7	E-422	Sunil	Sales	Exe.	20000	1000
8	E-304	Alia	Marketing	Exe.	20000	1000
9	E-345	Mukesh	Finance	Mgr	78000	3900
10	E-158	Ramakrish	Operations	Sr. Mgr	35000	1750
11	E-439	Divya	Finance	Exe.	22000	1100
12	E-323	Keshav	Sales	Sr. Mgr	35000	1750
13	E-267	Kunal	Sales	Mgr	58000	2900
14	E-297	Vijya	Admin	Sr. Mgr	30000	1500
15						

Figure 3.25

We will follow the steps to filter the data on the said condition:

1. Select the complete data including headers.

2. Under the Data tab select Filter. This will apply a drop-down list on each column header.

3. Click on the drop-down icon on the Emp. ID. column. Choose Filter by Color (Note: Filter by Color option is active because Excel has detected that this active column has cell/font colors). Then choose Filter by Cell's Color | Choose the respective color.

4. Click Ok.

5. Data will get filtered accordingly (see the following *Figure 3.26*):

	A	B	C	D	E	F
1			Employee Data			
2	Emp. ID	Name	Departme	Designati	Salary	Bonus
4	E-324	Deepak	Marketing	Exe.	18000	900
7	E-422	Sunil	Sales	Exe.	20000	1000
11	E-439	Divya	Finance	Exe.	22000	1100
14	E-297	Vijya	Admin	Sr. Mgr	30000	1500

Figure 3.26

Font Color Filter: Let's see how to filter data on the basis of font color. As shown in *Figure 3.27* below, some of the employee names are in red color font.

	A	B	C	D	E	F
1			Employee Data			
2	Emp. ID	Name	Department	Designation	Salary	Bonus
3	E-203	Arjun	Finance	Exe.	20000	1000
4	E-324	Deepak	Marketing	Exe.	18000	900
5	E-185	Anuj	Marketing	Mgr	55000	2750
6	E-270	Devaang	Finance	Sr. Mgr	32000	1600
7	E-422	Sunil	Sales	Exe.	20000	1000
8	E-304	Alia	Marketing	Exe.	20000	1000
9	E-345	Mukesh	Finance	Mgr	78000	3900
10	E-158	Ramakrish	Operations	Sr. Mgr	35000	1750
11	E-439	Divya	Finance	Exe.	22000	1100
12	E-323	Keshav	Sales	Sr. Mgr	35000	1750
13	E-267	Kunal	Sales	Mgr	58000	2900
14	E-297	Vijya	Admin	Sr. Mgr	30000	1500

Figure 3.27

1. Select the complete data including headers.

2. Under the Data tab select Filter. This will apply a drop-down list on each column header.

3. Click on the drop-down icon in the Name column. Choose Filter by Cell Color (Note: Filter by color option is active because Excel has detected that this active column has cell/font colors). Then choose Filter by Font Color and then choose the respective color.

4. Click Ok.

5. Data will get filtered accordingly (see the following *Figure 3.28*):

◢	A	B	C	D	E	F
1			Employee Data			
2	Emp. IC ▾	Name ▾	Departme ▾	Designati ▾	Salary ▾	Bonus ▾
4	E-324	Deepak	Marketing	Exe.	18000	900
7	E-422	Sunil	Sales	Exe.	20000	1000
10	E-158	Ramakris	Operations	Sr. Mgr	35000	1750
14	E-297	Vijya	Admin	Sr. Mgr	30000	1500

Figure 3.28

Applying Advanced Filter

Advanced filter is used when we have a set of complex criteria or more than one criteria on a single data field. The filter discussed in the previous section cannot accept two filtering criteria simultaneously (for example, showing employees whose salary is greater than 25000, along with those employees whose salary is between 25000 and 45000 and are from the sales department). Let's see how the Advanced filter can solve this problem.

Exercise file

A workbook containing the exercise files used in this chapter for Advanced Filtera in Excel, is available on https://rebrand.ly/ffdbc, the file is named 3.2 Advanced Filter.xlsx. You can download it and practice along.

Before enabling the Advanced filter option, first you need to create a Criteria Range, that is, a list of all the criteria, as shown in the following *Figure 3.29*:

16	Criteria Range					
17	Emp. ID	Name	Department	Designation	Salary	Bonus
18					<=25000	
19			Sales		<=45000	

Figure 3.29

Here, first the required headers is copied and then I have listed down both the conditions I had under respective column. One can create these criteria range anywhere in the sheet because a reference to be given in Advanced Filter option.

Follow the steps to apply the **Advanced Filter**:

1. Under the **Data** tab, select **Sort & Filter**, and then **Advanced Filter** (this will trigger a dialog box).

2. Under **List range**, select the complete data set including headers.

3. Under **Criteria range**, select the complete criteria range including header.

4. Select either **Filter the list, in-place** or **Copy to another location**. If you select the **Filter the list, in-place** option then Excel will filter the original database to show only those rows which match with the given criteria, whereas in the case of **Copy to another location**, you can assign a location, where the filtered data will be displayed and the original database will remain unaltered.

5. Check on **Unique records only** (if there are duplicate data records it's better to check this option to get only unique data) see the following *Figure 3.30*:

	A	B	C	D	E	F	G	H	I	J	K
1			Employee Data								
2	Emp. ID	Name	Department	Designation	Salary	Bonus					
3	E-203	Arjun	Finance	Exe.	20000	1000					
4	E-324	Deepak	Marketing	Exe.	18000	900					
5	E-185	Anuj	Marketing	Mgr	55000	2750			Advanced Filter ? ×		
6	E-270	Devaang	Finance	Sr. Mgr	32000	1600			Action		
7	E-422	Sunil	Sales	Exe.	20000	1000			○ Filter the list, in-place		
8	E-304	Alia	Marketing	Exe.	20000	1000			◉ Copy to another location		
9	E-345	Mukesh	Finance	Mgr	78000	3900			List range: $A$2:$F$14		
10	E-158	Ramakrish	Operations	Sr. Mgr	35000	1750			Criteria range: $A$17:$F$19		
11	E-439	Divya	Finance	Exe.	22000	1100			Copy to: ced Filter'!$I$2		
12	E-323	Keshav	Sales	Sr. Mgr	35000	1750					
13	E-267	Kunal	Sales	Mgr	58000	2900			☑ Unique records only		
14	E-297	Vijya	Admin	Sr. Mgr	30000	1500			OK Cancel		
15											
16	Criteria Range										
17	Emp. ID	Name	Department	Designation	Salary	Bonus					
18					<=25000						
19			Sales		<=45000						

Figure 3.30

6. Click **Ok**.

Filtered data will be displayed at the **Copy to another location**. See the following *Figure 3.31*:

Figure 3.31

The preceding outcome has all the records that match with the criteria listed in the Criteria Range.

Converting data into table

Excel offers a feature to convert any data set into a table format. Converting a data set into a table automatically turns on features like grand Total rows, AutoFilter and Sort, Banded Rows/Columns, and so on. It also helps to create additional columns or rows in a very easy manner. Using a simple data set, let's understand the features you get on converting it into a table.

Exercise file

A workbook containing the exercise files used in this chapter for Converting data into table in Excel, is available on https://rebrand.ly/ffdbc, the file is named 3.3 Converting data into table.xlsx. You can download it and practice along.

Creating a table

To convert a data set into a table follow these steps:

1. Select the data.

2. Under the Insert tab select Table. This will trigger a dialog box. Check on My table has headers see the following *Figure 3.32*:

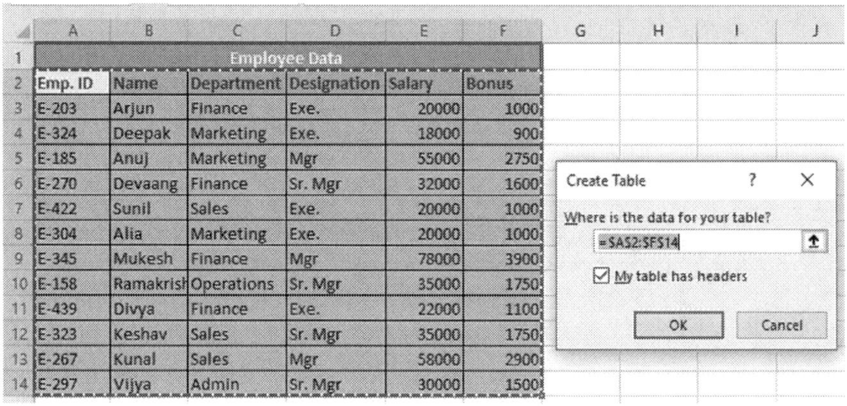

Emp. ID	Name	Department	Designation	Salary	Bonus
E-203	Arjun	Finance	Exe.	20000	1000
E-324	Deepak	Marketing	Exe.	18000	900
E-185	Anuj	Marketing	Mgr	55000	2750
E-270	Devaang	Finance	Sr. Mgr	32000	1600
E-422	Sunil	Sales	Exe.	20000	1000
E-304	Alia	Marketing	Exe.	20000	1000
E-345	Mukesh	Finance	Mgr	78000	3900
E-158	Ramakrisl	Operations	Sr. Mgr	35000	1750
E-439	Divya	Finance	Exe.	22000	1100
E-323	Keshav	Sales	Sr. Mgr	35000	1750
E-267	Kunal	Sales	Mgr	58000	2900
E-297	Vijya	Admin	Sr. Mgr	30000	1500

Figure 3.32

3. Click Ok.

Excel will auto apply a table style too. See the following *Figure 3.33*:

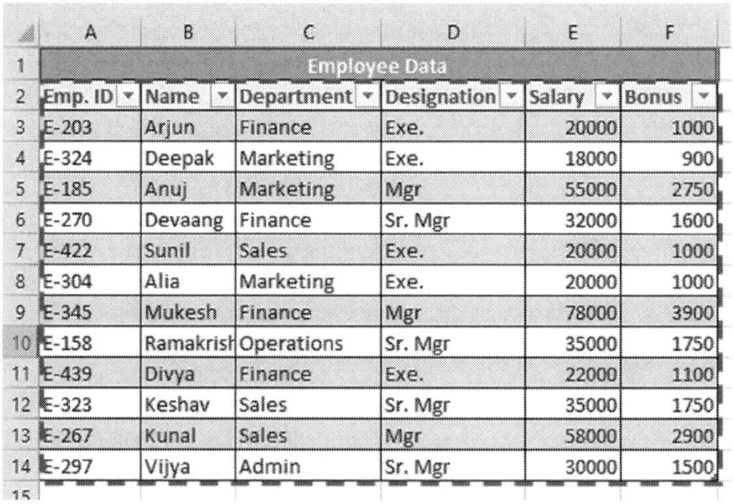

Emp. ID	Name	Department	Designation	Salary	Bonus
E-203	Arjun	Finance	Exe.	20000	1000
E-324	Deepak	Marketing	Exe.	18000	900
E-185	Anuj	Marketing	Mgr	55000	2750
E-270	Devaang	Finance	Sr. Mgr	32000	1600
E-422	Sunil	Sales	Exe.	20000	1000
E-304	Alia	Marketing	Exe.	20000	1000
E-345	Mukesh	Finance	Mgr	78000	3900
E-158	Ramakrisl	Operations	Sr. Mgr	35000	1750
E-439	Divya	Finance	Exe.	22000	1100
E-323	Keshav	Sales	Sr. Mgr	35000	1750
E-267	Kunal	Sales	Mgr	58000	2900
E-297	Vijya	Admin	Sr. Mgr	30000	1500

Figure 3.33

Choosing the correct design

As mentioned earlier, once you convert a data set into a table, Excel automatically applies a default table style. But you can change it in a snap. Whenever you use a table feature and if your active cell is somewhere in the table then Excel will display an additional section in the ribbon as Table Tools. See the following *Figure 3.34*:

ata into table.xlsx - Excel   Table Tools

eveloper   Help   Power Pivot   **Design**   ○ Tell i

☑ Header Row   ☐ First Column   ☑ Filter Button
☐ Total Row   ☐ Last Column
☑ Banded Rows ☐ Banded Columns

Table Style Options

Figure 3.34

Under the Table Tools tab, Select the Design tab and then Table Styles Options. You will find plenty of table styles to choose from. See the following *Figure 3.35*:

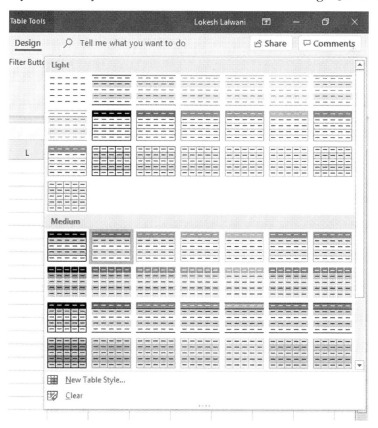

Figure 3.35

Here you can also create our own style using the New Table style option.

Note: If the data set is already formatted with Cell color, Font color or Border then converting it into a table will not overwrite the original formatting. So, first clear the formatting (under the Home tab select Font group) and then convert it into a table.

Adding columns and rows

In a table, adding a new column or row is a breeze. Just type the first instance of the new column or row and the Table format will detect that the user would like to add another column or row and will immediately assist us in the same and make it a part of the table. For example, in the sample data set, you want to create a column showing the taxes on each employee's salary. So, first enter the header of the column, Taxes, in cell G2 and hit *Enter*. As soon as you do so, Excel will make it a part of the table and apply all its handy features automatically (see the following *Figure 3.36*):

	A	B	C	D	E	F	G
1				Employee Data			
2	Emp. ID	Name	Department	Designation	Salary	Bonus	Taxes
3	E-203	Arjun	Finance	Exe.	20000	1000	
4	E-324	Deepak	Marketing	Exe.	18000	900	
5	E-185	Anuj	Marketing	Mgr	55000	2750	
6	E-270	Devaang	Finance	Sr. Mgr	32000	1600	
7	E-422	Sunil	Sales	Exe.	20000	1000	
8	E-304	Alia	Marketing	Exe.	20000	1000	
9	E-345	Mukesh	Finance	Mgr	78000	3900	
10	E-158	Ramakrish	Operations	Sr. Mgr	35000	1750	
11	E-439	Divya	Finance	Exe.	22000	1100	
12	E-323	Keshav	Sales	Sr. Mgr	35000	1750	
13	E-267	Kunal	Sales	Mgr	58000	2900	
14	E-297	Vijya	Admin	Sr. Mgr	30000	1500	

Figure 3.36

Next, set the first cell in the Taxes column, that is, cell G3, as 10% of the Salary column, that is, *=E3*10%*. As soon as you hit *Enter*, Excel will fill the entire column with the same calculation and will change the cell references accordingly (see the following *Figure 3.37* and *Figure 3.38*):

G3		× ✓	fx	=[@Salary]*10%				
	A	B	C	D	E	F	G	H
1				Employee Data				
2	Emp. ID	Name	Department	Designation	Salary	Bonus	Taxes	
3	E-203	Arjun	Finance	Exe.	20000	1000	=[@Salary]*10%	
4	E-324	Deepak	Marketing	Exe.	18000	900		
5	E-185	Anuj	Marketing	Mgr	55000	2750		
6	E-270	Devaang	Finance	Sr. Mgr	32000	1600		
7	E-422	Sunil	Sales	Exe.	20000	1000		
8	E-304	Alia	Marketing	Exe.	20000	1000		
9	E-345	Mukesh	Finance	Mgr	78000	3900		
10	E-158	Ramakrish	Operations	Sr. Mgr	35000	1750		
11	E-439	Divya	Finance	Exe.	22000	1100		
12	E-323	Keshav	Sales	Sr. Mgr	35000	1750		
13	E-267	Kunal	Sales	Mgr	58000	2900		
14	E-297	Vijya	Admin	Sr. Mgr	30000	1500		

Figure 3.37

Figure 3.38

Similar to a new column, you can also add a new row and Excel will automatically detect it and apply all the table features to it. As soon as you type the first instance in a row and hit the *Enter* or *Tab* key, Excel will create a new row automatically (see the following *Figure 3.39*):

Figure 3.39

Deleting columns or rows

The easiest way to delete a row or column is to just right click on it, go to the Delete menu, and then select Table column or Table row (see the following *Figure 3.40*):

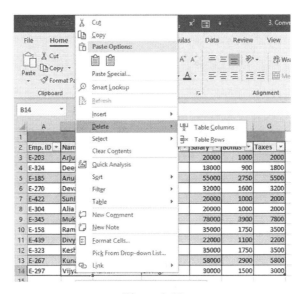

Figure 3.40

Enabling total row

When using the table format, Excel offers an option to sum up all the rows at the bottom of the table, thus eliminating the need to do so manually. To enable Total Row, place the cursor anywhere in the table, and then select the Table Tools section in the ribbon. Under the Design tab go to Table Style Options and check on the Total Row option (see the following *Figure 3.41*):

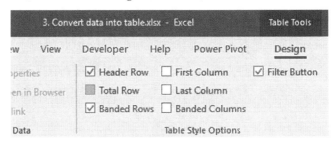

Figure 3.41

This will add a total row at the bottom of the table (see the following *Figure 3.42*):

	A	B	C	D	E	F	G
1			Employee Data				
2	Emp. ID	Name	Department	Designation	Salary	Bonus	Taxes
3	E-203	Arjun	Finance	Exe.	20000	1000	2000
4	E-324	Deepak	Marketing	Exe.	18000	900	1800
5	E-185	Anuj	Marketing	Mgr	55000	2750	5500
6	E-270	Devaang	Finance	Sr. Mgr	32000	1600	3200
7	E-422	Sunil	Sales	Exe.	20000	1000	2000
8	E-304	Alia	Marketing	Exe.	20000	1000	2000
9	E-345	Mukesh	Finance	Mgr	78000	3900	7800
10	E-158	Ramakrish	Operations	Sr. Mgr	35000	1750	3500
11	E-439	Divya	Finance	Exe.	22000	1100	2200
12	E-323	Keshav	Sales	Sr. Mgr	35000	1750	3500
13	E-267	Kunal	Sales	Mgr	58000	2900	5800
14	E-297	Vijya	Admin	Sr. Mgr	30000	1500	3000
15	Total				423000	21150	42300
16							

Figure 3.42

Sorting in a table

Sort feature is enabled the moment you apply a Table feature. As all the sorting features that have already been discussed in the beginning of this section are available here, it's just a matter of right-clicking on any cell of the column by which we would like to sort the table. For example, if you want that the complete table to be sorted by Salary in an ascending order then right-click on any cell of the Salary column, then select Sort, and then select Sort Smallest to Largest (see the following *Figure 3.43*):

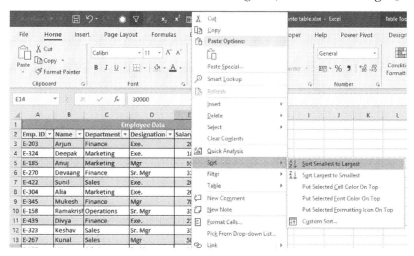

Figure 3.43

The table will get sorted as shown in the following *Figure 3.44*):

	A	B	C	D	E	F	G
1				Employee Data			
2	Emp. ID	Name	Department	Designation	Salary	Bonus	Taxes
3	E-324	Deepak	Marketing	Exe.	18000	900	1800
4	E-203	Arjun	Finance	Exe.	20000	1000	2000
5	E-422	Sunil	Sales	Exe.	20000	1000	2000
6	E-304	Alia	Marketing	Exe.	20000	1000	2000
7	E-439	Divya	Finance	Exe.	22000	1100	2200
8	E-297	Vijya	Admin	Sr. Mgr	30000	1500	3000
9	E-270	Devaang	Finance	Sr. Mgr	32000	1600	3200
10	E-158	Ramakrish	Operations	Sr. Mgr	35000	1750	3500
11	E-323	Keshav	Sales	Sr. Mgr	35000	1750	3500
12	E-185	Anuj	Marketing	Mgr	55000	2750	5500
13	E-267	Kunal	Sales	Mgr	58000	2900	5800
14	E-345	Mukesh	Finance	Mgr	78000	3900	7800
15	Total				423000	21150	42300

Figure 3.44

Filtering in a table

Filtering is also an easy task to perform in a table. So far you may have already noticed that the moment we convert a data set into a table, Excel automatically applies filter to the headers (see the following *Figure 3.45*):

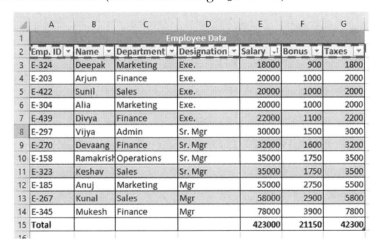

	A	B	C	D	E	F	G
1				Employee Data			
2	Emp. ID	Name	Department	Designation	Salary	Bonus	Taxes
3	E-324	Deepak	Marketing	Exe.	18000	900	1800
4	E-203	Arjun	Finance	Exe.	20000	1000	2000
5	E-422	Sunil	Sales	Exe.	20000	1000	2000
6	E-304	Alia	Marketing	Exe.	20000	1000	2000
7	E-439	Divya	Finance	Exe.	22000	1100	2200
8	E-297	Vijya	Admin	Sr. Mgr	30000	1500	3000
9	E-270	Devaang	Finance	Sr. Mgr	32000	1600	3200
10	E-158	Ramakrish	Operations	Sr. Mgr	35000	1750	3500
11	E-323	Keshav	Sales	Sr. Mgr	35000	1750	3500
12	E-185	Anuj	Marketing	Mgr	55000	2750	5500
13	E-267	Kunal	Sales	Mgr	58000	2900	5800
14	E-345	Mukesh	Finance	Mgr	78000	3900	7800
15	Total				423000	21150	42300
16							

Figure 3.45

Let's take an example where you want to see only the data for the Finance department employees. Follow the steps:

1. Click on the drop-down icon of the Department column.

2. Check only Finance and leave the rest of the items unchecked (see the following *Figure 3.46*):

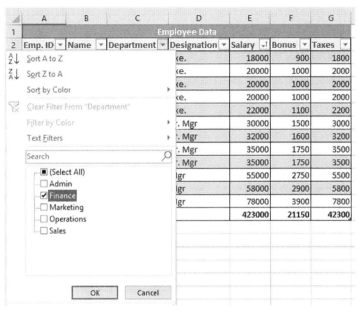

Figure 3.46

3. Click Ok.

Data will get filtered (see the following *Figure 3.47*):

	A	B	C	D	E	F	G
1				Employee Data			
2	Emp. ID ▼	Name ▼	Department ◢▼	Designation ▼	Salary ↓▼	Bonus ▼	Taxes ▼
4	E-203	Arjun	Finance	Exe.	20000	1000	2000
7	E-439	Divya	Finance	Exe.	22000	1100	2200
9	E-270	Devaang	Finance	Sr. Mgr	32000	1600	3200
14	E-345	Mukesh	Finance	Mgr	78000	3900	7800
15	Total				152000	7600	15200
16							

Figure 3.47

Converting header row to column title

This is another amazing feature of an Excel table, where it automatically converts the header row to column title as you scroll down, thus helping you keep track of the column label (see the following *Figure 3.48*):

	Emp. ID ▾	Name ▾	Department ▾	Designation ▾	Salary ▾	Bonus ▾	Taxes ▾
10	E-158	Ramakrish	Operations	Sr. Mgr	35000	1750	3500
11	E-323	Keshav	Sales	Sr. Mgr	35000	1750	3500
12	E-185	Anuj	Marketing	Mgr	55000	2750	5500
13	E-267	Kunal	Sales	Mgr	58000	2900	5800
14	E-345	Mukesh	Finance	Mgr	78000	3900	7800
15	Total				423000	21150	42300

Figure 3.48

Reconverting table to data set

A table can be reconverted to a data set again in a single click. Following steps will do the job:

1. Keep the cursor in the table area.

2. Under the Table Tools section in ribbon, select the Design tab, then Tools, and then Convert to Range. This step will trigger an information dialog box, asking your permission for the same see the following *Figure 3.49*:

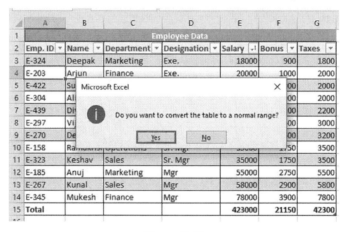

Figure 3.49

3. Click Ok.

Our table is now back to a normal data set (see the following *Figure 3.50*).

Note: Any changes made to the table will still be retained.

	A	B	C	D	E	F	G
1				Employee Data			
2	Emp. ID	Name	Department	Designation	Salary	Bonus	Taxes
3	E-324	Deepak	Marketing	Exe.	18000	900	1800
4	E-203	Arjun	Finance	Exe.	20000	1000	2000
5	E-422	Sunil	Sales	Exe.	20000	1000	2000
6	E-304	Alia	Marketing	Exe.	20000	1000	2000
7	E-439	Divya	Finance	Exe.	22000	1100	2200
8	E-297	Vijya	Admin	Sr. Mgr	30000	1500	3000
9	E-270	Devaang	Finance	Sr. Mgr	32000	1600	3200
10	E-158	Ramakrish	Operations	Sr. Mgr	35000	1750	3500
11	E-323	Keshav	Sales	Sr. Mgr	35000	1750	3500
12	E-185	Anuj	Marketing	Mgr	55000	2750	5500
13	E-267	Kunal	Sales	Mgr	58000	2900	5800
14	E-345	Mukesh	Finance	Mgr	78000	3900	7800
15	Total				423000	21150	42300

Figure 3.50

Protecting Worksheet and/or Workbook

At times it's important to protect our worksheets and workbooks with a password to restrict its access to the intended user. Let's seehow it's done for worksheets and workbooks one by one.

Worksheet – protect and unprotect

Protect: This feature helps us protect the contents of a worksheet. As it's worksheet level protection, all the objects in the sheet can be protected. When a worksheet is not protected, every cell in the sheet is already Locked. So, once you protect the sheet using a password, each and every cell in the sheet will get protected. To check the status of a cell, that is, whether it is locked or unlocked, right-click on any cell. Then under Format Cells, select the Protection tab. See the following *Figure 3.51*:

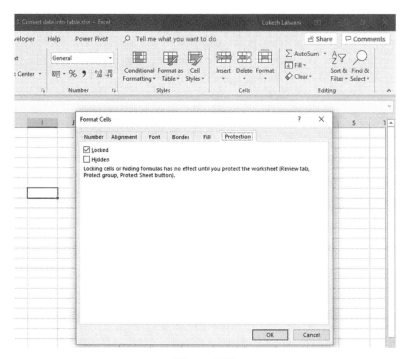

Figure 3.51

Let's follow the below steps to apply worksheet level protection:

1. Activate the sheet you want to protect by clicking anywhere in it.

2. Under the **Review** tab, go to **Protect** group and select **Protect Sheet**. This will trigger a dialog box as shown in the following *Figure 3.52*:

Figure 3.52

Note: "Allow all users of this worksheet to:" is a list of permissions that can be given to a user. Whatever is checked in the list is permitted. For example, currently "Select locked cells" and "Select unlocked cells" are checked. This means that once you share this file with a user, they will be able to select both "Locked" and "Unlocked" cells but they won't be able to edit any "Locked" cells until they unprotect the sheet. So, let's keep it unchanged here.

3. Enter a Password, and click Ok. Then re-enter the same password and again click Ok.

Now when you try to edit any cell in the worksheet, Excel will immediately open the below dialog box (see the following *Figure 3.53*):

Figure 3.53

Unprotect: To unprotect a worksheet follow the steps:

1. Activate the sheet you want to unprotect by clicking anywhere in it.

2. Under the Review tab, go to Protect group, and select Unprotect Sheet. This will trigger a dialog box asking for the password see *Figure 3.54*:

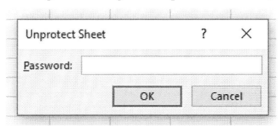

Figure 3.54

3. Enter the password and click Ok.

The sheet will be unprotected now.

Workbook – Protect and unprotect

Protect: Workbook protection can have two further levels of protection, that is, one is for the opening the workbook and the other level is for opening it in a read-only manner. Let's understand these levels of protection by following the steps:

1. Under the File tab, select Save As, and then Browse. This will open up a dialog box as shown in the following *Figure 3.55*:

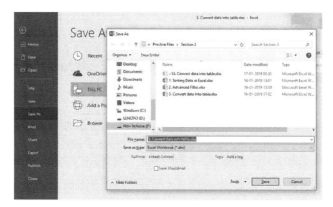

Figure 3.55

2. In the drop-down list of **Tools** select **General Options...** (see the following *Figure 3.56*):

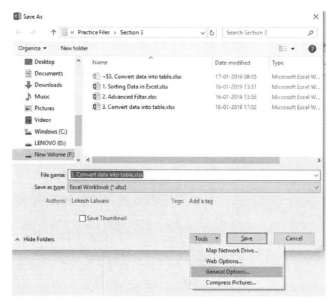

Figure 3.56

3. You can either select **Password to open** or **Password to modify** or both (see the following *Figure 3.57*):

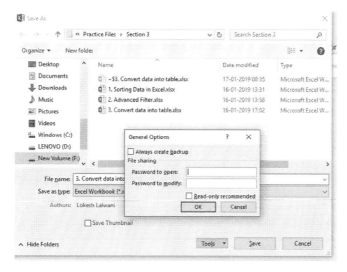

Figure 3.57

4. Once you set the password, click Ok and save a copy of this file in a preferred location. Now if you try to open this protected workbook, it will ask for the password (see the following *Figure 3.58*):

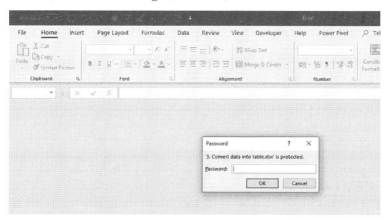

Figure 3.58

Excel will open the workbook only when the user enters the correct password. As in this example we have set **Password to modify** also, entering the correct password here will open the workbook but will not allow editing until the user enter a correct password for **Password to modify** (see the following *Figure 3.59*):

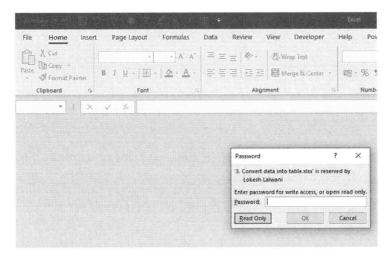

Figure 3.59

Unprotect: To unprotect a workbook, you need to follow the same steps as you used to protect it and then simply delete the passwords from the dialog box where you had entered them earlier.Finally save a copy of the same at a preferred location (see the following *Figure 3.60*):

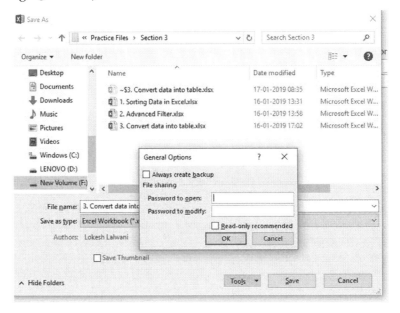

Figure 3.60

Summary

Data transformation and management are a fundamental concept in data analysis. As we have seen in this chapter, Excel provides amazing tools (such as Sort and Filter to arrange and slice data, Advanced filter to filter data on the basis of complex conditions, converting raw data into a table to transform data from a raw format to an organized format. Excel provides some security options to protect your sensitive information on worksheet and workbook level.

Once the data is transformed it's time to apply various formulas and functions. These functions will help us further in analyzing the data. Excel provides various functions like Text, Statistical, Financial, Date and Time, Conditional, Lookup, and so on. Let's explore them in detail with practical examples in the next chapter.

CHAPTER 4

Formulas and Functions

Calculations, formulas, and functions are at the heart of Excel program. To perform a calculation, an Excel user can either write a formula or use a built-in function. Formulas are all about using mathematical operators such as "+", "-", "*",and so on, and symbols to perform calculations, while functions are built-in formulas with a label. Most Excel users prefer to use a formula or function as a label for both manually written and built-in calculation expression.

In this chapter, we will discuss:

- Writing Excel formulas and functions
- Basic functions (such as sum, count, average, etc.)
- Conditional calculations (SUMIF, COUNTIF, AVERAGEIF, etc.)
- Logical functions
- Text functions (TRIM, FIND, SEARCH, etc.)
- Date and time functions
- Lookup functions (VLOOKUP, HLOOKUP, INDEX, MATCH, etc.)

Objective:

After reading this chapter, you will be able to understand the basics of formula and function writing in Excel. You will be able to perform calculations such as Sum, Count, and Average based on certain conditions. You will be equipped with the knowledge of various Text functions used to clean data. Providing knowledge on various Date & Time functions is also an objective of this section. In addition, you will learn various logical functions such as IF, AND, and OR. Finally, this chapter will provide you in-depth knowledge on some of the most useful functions, that is, Lookup & Reference functions like VLOOKUP, HLOOKUP, MATCH, and so on.

Writing Excel formulas and functions

Formulas use calculation operators such as +, -, *, and /. Whether it's a formula or a function, always start with the"=" is equal to symbol.

Exercise file

A workbook containing the exercise files used in this chapter for Write your first Formula in Excel, is available on https://rebrand.ly/ffdbc, the file is named 4.1 Write your first Formula.xlsx. You can download it and practice along.

Summing values

Let's adopt a practical approach. Here we have a small data set of products and their sales across multiple locations see the following *Figure 4.1*:

	A	B	C	D	E	F
	Sales Data					
1						
2	Prodcuts	Delhi	Mumbai	Kolkata	Total Sales	
3	A	500	608	597		
4	B	833	646	811		
5	C	515	900	566		
6	D	965	993	643		
7	E	889	579	520		
8	F	545	738	766		
9						

Figure 4.1

Let's find the total sales for each product by summing the entries in the respective rows. This can be done using the + symbol, but there are two ways to perform such a calculation.

1. You can write a formula to sum the sales for product A as = 500+608+597, which will give you a correct outcome but there are two drawbacks in this approach:

    • You can't copy and paste this formula to get the sum of all the products.

- If any of the sales amount changes, then the result, that is, sum will not change accordingly.

2. You can write the formula by referring to the cells containing the sales amount, for example, =B3+C3+D3. This will overcome the preceding two drawbacks. See the following *Figure 4.2*:

	A	B	C	D	E
1			Sales Data		
2	Prodcuts	Delhi	Mumbai	Kolkata	Total Sales
3	A	500	608	597	=B3+C3+D3
4	B	833	646	811	
5	C	515	900	566	
6	D	965	993	643	
7	E	889	579	520	
8	F	545	738	766	

Figure 4.2

Thus, it's better to use the second method to perform calculations.

Subtracting values

Consider a data set containing product wise sales and cost to find the profit per product. See the following *Figure 4.3*:

	A	B	C	D
1		Sales Data		
2	Prodcuts	Revenue	Cost	Profit
3	A	500	450	
4	B	833	700	
5	C	515	485	
6	D	965	966	
7	E	889	812	
8	F	545	491	
9				

Figure 4.3

Again, you can use the - sign to subtract the values and get the profit. For example, to find out the profit for product A, you can write the formula as =B3-C3. See the following *Figure 4.4*:

◢	A	B	C	D
1		Sales Data		
2	Prodcuts	Revenue	Cost	Profit
3	A	500	450	=B3-C3
4	B	833	700	
5	C	515	485	
6	D	965	966	
7	E	889	812	
8	F	545	491	

Figure 4.4

You can further copy and paste this formula to find the profit or loss for the rest of the products.

Rest of the calculations such as "/" division, "*" multiplication, "%" percentage, "^" and exponential can be performed similarly.

Functions

A function is a pre-defined formula assigned to a respective label that has its own syntax and arguments. You can follow the arguments mentioned in the syntax of the function to get the desired output.

Understanding syntax and arguments

Every function has its own syntax and every syntax has its own arguments. Excel has over 200 built-in functions, and so it's next to impossible to memorize their syntax and arguments. Nonetheless, once you learn the important logic for each syntax, it is very easy to write almost any function in Excel.

So let's understand how to write a function in Excel. *Figure 4.5* below shows invoice numbers, office location, and the invoice amount. We will apply the SUM function and understand its syntax and arguments of this function:

Exercise file

A workbook containing the exercise files used in this chapter for Function writing in Excel, is available on https://rebrand.ly/ffdbc the file is named 4.2 Function writing.xlsx. You can download it and practice along.

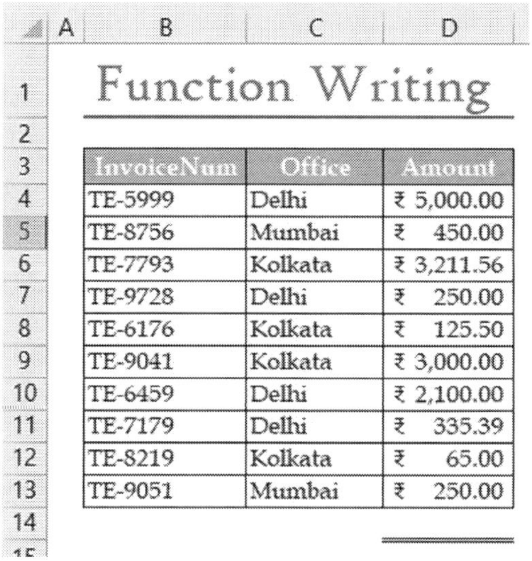

Function Writing

InvoiceNum	Office	Amount
TE-5999	Delhi	₹ 5,000.00
TE-8756	Mumbai	₹ 450.00
TE-7793	Kolkata	₹ 3,211.56
TE-9728	Delhi	₹ 250.00
TE-6176	Kolkata	₹ 125.50
TE-9041	Kolkata	₹ 3,000.00
TE-6459	Delhi	₹ 2,100.00
TE-7179	Delhi	₹ 335.39
TE-8219	Kolkata	₹ 65.00
TE-9051	Mumbai	₹ 250.00

Figure 4.5

Let's apply the SUM function in cell D14. Start by writing the function as =SUM. Then you can either press the *Tab* key or select the function from the list by left-clicking the mouse twice. Excel will open the function, with an opening parenthesis, and show the syntax seen in the following *Figure 4.6*:

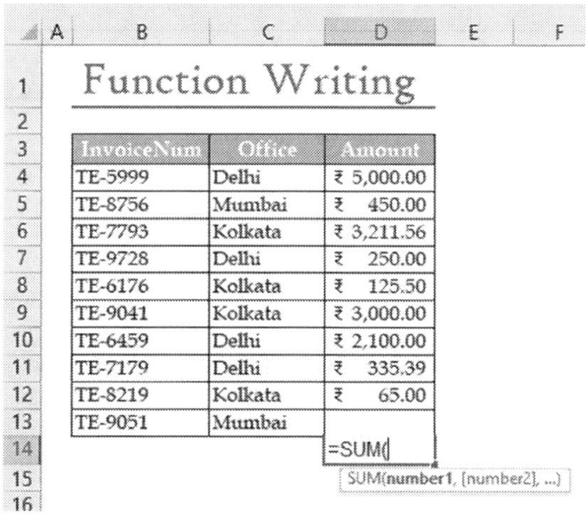

Function Writing

InvoiceNum	Office	Amount
TE-5999	Delhi	₹ 5,000.00
TE-8756	Mumbai	₹ 450.00
TE-7793	Kolkata	₹ 3,211.56
TE-9728	Delhi	₹ 250.00
TE-6176	Kolkata	₹ 125.50
TE-9041	Kolkata	₹ 3,000.00
TE-6459	Delhi	₹ 2,100.00
TE-7179	Delhi	₹ 335.39
TE-8219	Kolkata	₹ 65.00
TE-9051	Mumbai	
		=SUM(

Figure 4.6

Syntax:

Sum(number1, [number2],...)

- number1: This argument is in bold font indicating that this argument is active right now.

- [number2]: This argument is in square brackets indicating that this argument is optional, that is, even if you omit this argument, the function will still give you the result based on previous arguments.

Note: It's always important to remember that number1, number2, **etc. are just labels to an argument. It doesn't mean that the argument can have only one number; it can contain a range also, and a range can contain multiple cells.**

Consider the example below, where instead of filling up each argument one by one, we will use a complete range having all the amounts.

See the following *Figure 4.7*:

	InvoiceNum	Office	Amount
4	TE-5999	Delhi	₹ 5,000.00
5	TE-8756	Mumbai	₹ 450.00
6	TE-7793	Kolkata	₹ 3,211.56
7	TE-9728	Delhi	₹ 250.00
8	TE-6176	Kolkata	₹ 125.50
9	TE-9041	Kolkata	₹ 3,000.00
10	TE-6459	Delhi	₹ 2,100.00
11	TE-7179	Delhi	₹ 335.39
12	TE-8219	Kolkata	₹ 65.00
13	TE-9051	Mumbai	

=SUM(D4:D13|

SUM(**number1**, [number2], ...)

10R x 1C

Figure 4.7

This way we can sum a set of million numbers by using only one argument. Hit *Enter* and you will get the sum (see the following *Figure 4.8*). As you may have guessed, the sum will change whenever you edit any value in the range:

	InvoiceNum	Office	Amount
4	TE-5999	Delhi	₹ 5,000.00
5	TE-8756	Mumbai	₹ 450.00
6	TE-7793	Kolkata	₹ 3,211.56
7	TE-9728	Delhi	₹ 250.00
8	TE-6176	Kolkata	₹ 125.50
9	TE-9041	Kolkata	₹ 3,000.00
10	TE-6459	Delhi	₹ 2,100.00
11	TE-7179	Delhi	₹ 335.39
12	TE-8219	Kolkata	₹ 65.00
13	TE-9051	Mumbai	₹ 250.00
14			₹ 14,787.45

Figure 4.8

Basic calculations

You now know the basic difference between a formula and a function, although you can use these terms interchangeably. Here onwards, you will feel a great need to apply basic calculation functions such as:

- Sum
- Count functions (COUNT, CountA, CountBlank)
- Average
- Max
- Min

Let's understand these functions in detail and then we will move forward towards some advanced functions. We have already discussed the SUM function, so now let's cover the rest of the functions individually.

COUNT functions (COUNT, CountA, CountBlank)

To simply count the cells without any condition, use the following functions in Excel:

COUNT

The COUNT function can count only those cells that contain numeric values.

Syntax:

COUNT(value1, [value2], ...)

- value1: This is the required argument. The first item, cell reference, or range within which you want to count numbers.

- value2: This is an optional argument. Up to 255 additional items, cell references, or ranges within which you want to count numbers.

Let's use the same example as previously. You can apply the COUNT function only on the Amount column. See the following *Figure 4.9*:

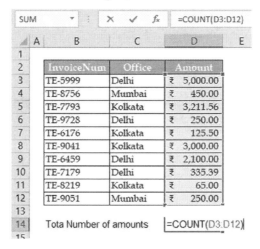

Figure 4.9

COUNTA

This function count cells that contains numbers as well as text.

Syntax:

COUNTA(value1, [value2], ...)

- value1: This is the required argument. The first argument representing the values you want to count.

- value2: This is the optional argument. These are Additional arguments representing the values that you want to count, up to a maximum of 255 arguments.

Using the same database again, you can apply this function to any of the columns to get a count of cells. See the following *Figure 4.10*:

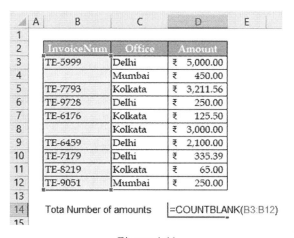

Figure 4.10

COUNTBLANK

This function can count all the blank cells in a range. This is useful especially in the case of a large data set.

Syntax:

COUNTBLANK(range)

- range: This is the required argument. The range in which you want to count the blank cells.

Let's take an example, of a data set with some blank cells. See the following *Figure 4.11*:

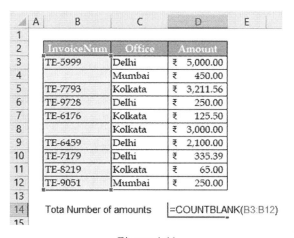

Figure 4.11

Conditional calculation

When working on a data set in real life, things are not as straight forward as discussed in previous examples We are required to analyze data on the basis of certain conditions. In Excel, condition stands for IF. Excel provides us some really smart conditional calculation functions. For example, to calculate sum on the basis of certain condition, you can use SUMIF or SUMIFS. Let's explore them.

Exercise file

A workbook containing the exercise files used in this chapter for Conditional Calculation in Excel, is available on https://rebrand.ly/ffdbc, the file is named 4.3 Conditional Calculation.xlsx. You can download it and practice along.

SUMIF

This is one of the most useful functions in Excel. It is used to sum values on the basis of certain conditions (e.g., total sales for a particular region, total expenses in one branch of a company, total salary paid to a particular department, and so on.

Syntax:

SUMIF(range, criteria, [sum_range])

- range: This is the required argument. This is the range of cells you want evaluated by criteria. The cells in this range must have numbers or names, arrays, or references that contain numbers. Blank and text values are ignored. The selected range may contain dates in standard Excel format (following examples).

- Criteria: This is the required argument. This in the form of a number, an expression, a cell reference, text, or a function that defines which cells will be added. For example, criteria can be expressed as 32, ">32", B5, "32", "apples", or TODAY().

- sum_range: This is an optional argument. This is used to specify the actual cells you want to add, if you want to add cells other than those specified in the range argument. If the sum_range argument is omitted, Excel adds the cells that are specified in the range argument (the same cells to which the criteria is applied).

You can use wildcard characters, such as the question mark (?) and asterisk (*), as the criteria argument. A question mark matches any single character; an asterisk matches any sequence of characters. If you want to find an actual question mark or asterisk, type a tilde (~) preceding the character.

Let's again consider the previous example. Here, let's sum the amount of only those invoices that belongs to Delhi office. See the following *Figure 4.12*:

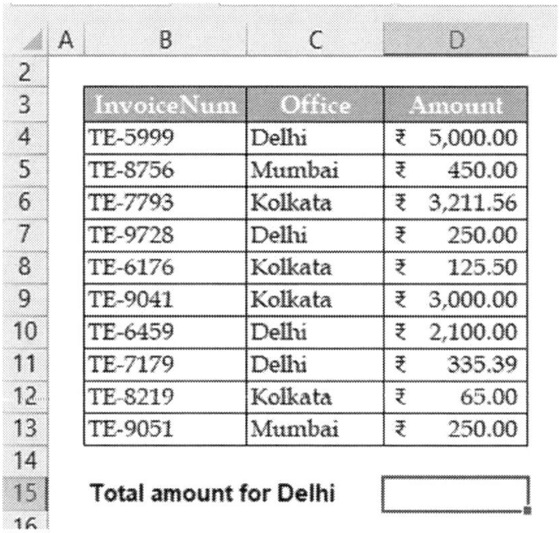

Figure 4.12

The function will be written shown in the following *Figure 4.13*:

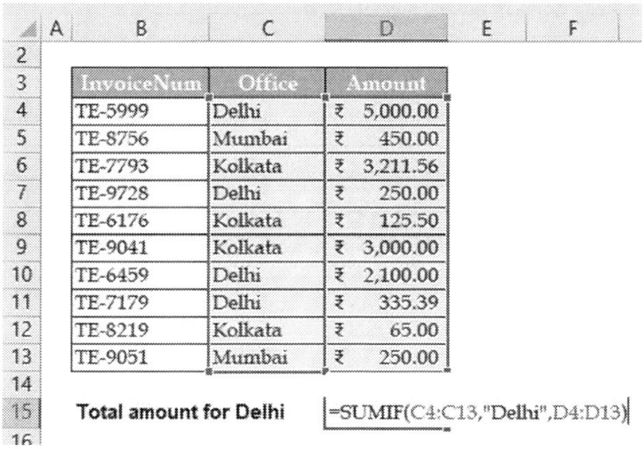

Figure 4.13

Note: Criteria is written in double quotes ("Delhi") because it's a text. Instead of writing "Delhi", you could have also selected a cell containing Delhi, for example, cell C4 or C7, and so on but without the double quotes "".

SUMIFS

Unlike SUMIF, SUMIFS can support more than one criteria/condition.

Syntax:

SUMIFS(sum_range, criteria_range1, criteria1, [criteria_range2, criteria2], ...)

- sum_range: This is the required argument. This is the range of cells to sum.

- criteria_range1: This is the required argument. This range is tested using criteria1. The criteria_range1 and criteria1 set up a search pair whereby a range is searched for specific criteria. Once the items in the range are found, their corresponding values in sum_range are added.

- criteria1: This is the required argument. This criteria defines which cells in criteria_range1 will be added. For example, criteria can be entered as 32, ">32", B4, apples, or "32".

- criteria_range2, criteria2: This is the optional argument. These are additional ranges and their associated criteria. You can enter up to 127 range/criteria pairs.

Let's understand this function through an example. We will sum only those amounts that belong to Delhi and are for product Bike. See the following *Figure 4.14*:

	A	B	C	D	E
1					
2		InvoiceNum	Office	Product	Amount
3		TE-5999	Delhi	Bike	₹ 5,000.00
4		TE-8756	Mumbai	Bike	₹ 450.00
5		TE-7793	Kolkata	Bike	₹ 3,211.56
6		TE-9728	Delhi	Accessories	₹ 250.00
7		TE-6176	Kolkata	Accessories	₹ 125.50
8		TE-9041	Kolkata	Bike	₹ 3,000.00
9		TE-6459	Delhi	Accessories	₹ 2,100.00
10		TE-7179	Delhi	Bike	₹ 335.39
11		TE-8219	Kolkata	Accessories	₹ 65.00
12		TE-9051	Mumbai	Bike	₹ 250.00
13					
14		**Total amount for Bike in Delhi**			
15					

Figure 4.14

The formula will look like the following *Figure 4.15*:

	A	B	C	D	E	F	G	H	I
	E14		× ✓ *fx*	=SUMIFS(E3:E12,C3:C12,"Delhi",D3:D12,"Bike")					
1									
2		InvoiceNum	Office	Product	Amount				
3		TE-5999	Delhi	Bike	₹ 5,000.00				
4		TE-8756	Mumbai	Bike	₹ 450.00				
5		TE-7793	Kolkata	Bike	₹ 3,211.56				
6		TE-9728	Delhi	Accessories	₹ 250.00				
7		TE-6176	Kolkata	Accessories	₹ 125.50				
8		TE-9041	Kolkata	Bike	₹ 3,000.00				
9		TE-6459	Delhi	Accessories	₹ 2,100.00				
10		TE-7179	Delhi	Bike	₹ 335.39				
11		TE-8219	Kolkata	Accessories	₹ 65.00				
12		TE-9051	Mumbai	Bike	₹ 250.00				
13									
14		**Total amount for Bike in Delhi**			=SUMIFS(E3:E12,C3:C12,"Delhi",D3:D12,"Bike")				

Figure 4.15

COUNTIF

This function is used to count cells on the basis of only one condition.

Syntax:

COUNTIF(range, criteria)

- range: This is the required argument. This is the group of cells you want to count. It can contain numbers, arrays, a named range, or references that contain numbers. Blank and text values are ignored.

- criteria: This is the required argument. This is a number, an expression, a cell reference, or a text string that determines which cells will be counted.

For example, you can use a number such as 32, an expressions such as ">32", a cell reference such as B4, or a text string such asapples.

COUNTIF uses only a single criteria. Use COUNTIFS if you want to use multiple criteria.

Here we have the same set of invoices and now let's count only those invoices that belongs to Delhi. See the following *Figure 4.16*:

InvoiceNum	Office	Amount
TE-5999	Delhi	₹ 5,000.00
TE-8756	Mumbai	₹ 450.00
TE-7793	Kolkata	₹ 3,211.56
TE-9728	Delhi	₹ 250.00
TE-6176	Kolkata	₹ 125.50
TE-9041	Kolkata	₹ 3,000.00
TE-6459	Delhi	₹ 2,100.00
TE-7179	Delhi	₹ 335.39
TE-8219	Kolkata	₹ 65.00
TE-9051	Mumbai	₹ 250.00

Total number of Invoices belongs to Delhi

Figure 4.16

When you apply COUNTIF, the function will look the following *Figure 4.17*):

InvoiceNum	Office	Amount
TE-5999	Delhi	₹ 5,000.00
TE-8756	Mumbai	₹ 450.00
TE-7793	Kolkata	₹ 3,211.56
TE-9728	Delhi	₹ 250.00
TE-6176	Kolkata	₹ 125.50
TE-9041	Kolkata	₹ 3,000.00
TE-6459	Delhi	₹ 2,100.00
TE-7179	Delhi	₹ 335.39
TE-8219	Kolkata	₹ 65.00
TE-9051	Mumbai	₹ 250.00

Total number of Invoices belongs to Delhi =COUNTIF(C4:C13,"delhi")

Figure 4.17

COUNTIFS

Use this function to count cells on the basis of more than one condition.

Syntax:

COUNTIFS(criteria_range1, criteria1, [criteria_range2, criteria2]...)

- criteria_range1: This is the required argument. This is the first range in which to evaluate the associated criteria.

- criteria1: This is the required argument. This is criteria in the form of a number, an expression, a cell reference, or a text that defines which cells will be counted. For example, criteria can be expressed as 32, ">32", B4, apples, or 32.

- criteria_range2, criteria2: This is the optional argument. These are additional ranges and their associated criteria. Up to 127 range/criteria pairs are allowed.

Using the previous example, let's now count the total number of invoices for product Bike at Delhi office. See the following *Figure 4.18*:

	A	B	C	D	E
1					
2		InvoiceNum	Office	Product	Amount
3		TE-5999	Delhi	Bike	₹ 5,000.00
4		TE-8756	Mumbai	Bike	₹ 450.00
5		TE-7793	Kolkata	Bike	₹ 3,211.56
6		TE-9728	Delhi	Accessories	₹ 250.00
7		TE-6176	Kolkata	Accessories	₹ 125.50
8		TE-9041	Kolkata	Bike	₹ 3,000.00
9		TE-6459	Delhi	Accessories	₹ 2,100.00
10		TE-7179	Delhi	Bike	₹ 335.39
11		TE-8219	Kolkata	Accessories	₹ 65.00
12		TE-9051	Mumbai	Bike	₹ 250.00
13					
14		Total number of invoices belongs to			
15		"Delhi" and are only for "Bike"			
16					

Figure 4.18

The function will look like the following *Figure 4.19*:

E14		× ✓ *fx*	=COUNTIFS(C3:C12,"Delhi",D3:D12,"Bike")					
	A	B	C	D	E	F	G	H
1								
2		InvoiceNum	Office	Product	Amount			
3		TE-5999	Delhi	Bike	₹ 5,000.00			
4		TE-8756	Mumbai	Bike	₹ 450.00			
5		TE-7793	Kolkata	Bike	₹ 3,211.56			
6		TE-9728	Delhi	Accessories	₹ 250.00			
7		TE-6176	Kolkata	Accessories	₹ 125.50			
8		TE-9041	Kolkata	Bike	₹ 3,000.00			
9		TE-6459	Delhi	Accessories	₹ 2,100.00			
10		TE-7179	Delhi	Bike	₹ 335.39			
11		TE-8219	Kolkata	Accessories	₹ 65.00			
12		TE-9051	Mumbai	Bike	₹ 250.00			
13								
14		Total number of invoices belongs to		=COUNTIFS(C3:C12,"Delhi",D3:D12,"Bike")				
15		"Delhi" and are only for "Bike"						

Figure 4.19

AVERAGEIF

Similar to previous calculations, average can also be calculated on the basis of certain condition.

Syntax:

AVERAGEIF(range, criteria, [average_range])

- range: This is the required argument. This is the range of one or more cells to average, including numbers or names, arrays, or references that contain numbers.

- Criteria: This is the required argument. This is criteria in the form of a number, an expression, a cell reference, or a text that defines which cells are averaged. For example, criteria can be expressed as 32, "32", ">32", apples, or B4.

- Average_range (Optional). This is used to specify the actual set of cells to be averaged. If omitted, range is used.

Let's calculate the average invoice amount for the Kolkata office. See the following *Figure 4.20*:

	A	B	C	D	
2					
3		InvoiceNum	Office	Amount	
4		TE-5999	Delhi	₹ 5,000.00	
5		TE-8756	Mumbai	₹ 450.00	
6		TE-7793	Kolkata	₹ 3,211.56	
7		TE-9728	Delhi	₹ 250.00	
8		TE-6176	Kolkata	₹ 125.50	
9		TE-9041	Kolkata	₹ 3,000.00	
10		TE-6459	Delhi	₹ 2,100.00	
11		TE-7179	Delhi	₹ 335.39	
12		TE-8219	Kolkata	₹ 65.00	
13		TE-9051	Mumbai	₹ 250.00	
14					
15		**Average amount of**			
16		**invoice for Kolkata**			
17					

Figure 4.20

The function for calculating the average will look as shown in *Figure 4.21*:

	A	B	C	D	E	F	G
2							
3		**InvoiceNum**	**Office**	**Amount**			
4		TE-5999	Delhi	₹ 5,000.00			
5		TE-8756	Mumbai	₹ 450.00			
6		TE-7793	Kolkata	₹ 3,211.56			
7		TE-9728	Delhi	₹ 250.00			
8		TE-6176	Kolkata	₹ 125.50			
9		TE-9041	Kolkata	₹ 3,000.00			
10		TE-6459	Delhi	₹ 2,100.00			
11		TE-7179	Delhi	₹ 335.39			
12		TE-8219	Kolkata	₹ 65.00			
13		TE-9051	Mumbai	₹ 250.00			
14							
15		**Average amount of**		=AVERAGEIF(C4:C13,"kolkata",D4:D13)			
16		**invoice for Kolkata**					
17							

Figure 4.21

Averageifs

Using this function for calculating average on the basis of more than one condition/criteria.

Syntax

AVERAGEIFS(average_range, criteria_range1, criteria1, [criteria_range2, criteria2], ...)

- average_range: This is the required argument. This is the range of one or more cells to average, including numbers or names, arrays, or references that contain numbers.

- Criteria_range1, criteria_range2: criteria_range1 is required, while the subsequent criteria_ranges are optional. There are 1 to 127 ranges in which to evaluate the associated criteria.

- criteria1, criteria2: criteria1 is required, and subsequent criteria are optional. There are 1 to 127 criteria in the form of a number, an expression, a cell reference, or text that define which cells will be averaged. For example, criteria can be expressed as 32, "32", ">32", apples, or B4.

Let's calculate the average invoice amount for Accessories at the Kolkata office using AVERAGEIFS. See the following *Figure 4.22*:

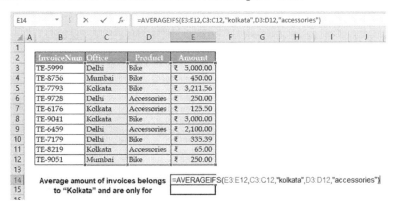

	A	B	C	D	E
2		InvoiceNum	Office	Product	Amount
3		TE-5999	Delhi	Bike	₹ 5,000.00
4		TE-8756	Mumbai	Bike	₹ 450.00
5		TE-7793	Kolkata	Bike	₹ 3,211.56
6		TE-9728	Delhi	Accessories	₹ 250.00
7		TE-6176	Kolkata	Accessories	₹ 125.50
8		TE-9041	Kolkata	Bike	₹ 3,000.00
9		TE-6459	Delhi	Accessories	₹ 2,100.00
10		TE-7179	Delhi	Bike	₹ 335.39
11		TE-8219	Kolkata	Accessories	₹ 65.00
12		TE-9051	Mumbai	Bike	₹ 250.00

Average amount of invoices belongs to "Kolkata" and are only for

Figure 4.22

The function for the same will look as shown in *Figure 4.23*:

E14 : × ✓ *fx* =AVERAGEIFS(E3:E12,C3:C12,"kolkata",D3:D12,"accessories")

	A	B	C	D	E	F	G	H	I	J
2		InvoiceNum	Office	Product	Amount					
3		TE-5999	Delhi	Bike	₹ 5,000.00					
4		TE-8756	Mumbai	Bike	₹ 450.00					
5		TE-7793	Kolkata	Bike	₹ 3,211.56					
6		TE-9728	Delhi	Accessories	₹ 250.00					
7		TE-6176	Kolkata	Accessories	₹ 125.50					
8		TE-9041	Kolkata	Bike	₹ 3,000.00					
9		TE-6459	Delhi	Accessories	₹ 2,100.00					
10		TE-7179	Delhi	Bike	₹ 335.39					
11		TE-8219	Kolkata	Accessories	₹ 65.00					
12		TE-9051	Mumbai	Bike	₹ 250.00					

Average amount of invoices belongs to "Kolkata" and are only for =AVERAGEIFS(E3:E12,C3:C12,"kolkata",D3:D12,"accessories")

Figure 4.23

Logical functions

These functions are the backbone of Excel, and are used to assign status on the basis of certain conditions. Further, calculation can also be done depending on the status. Let's dive in the world of logical functions and explore them one by one.

Exercise file

A workbook containing the exercise files used in this chapter for logical functions in Excel, is available on https://rebrand.ly/ffdbc, the file is named 4.4 Logical functions.xlsx. You can download it and practice along.

IF

This function is all about either this or that based on certain condition. For example, if you choose heads when a coin is tossed, and it lands showing heads up, win, else you lose, this is an IF condition.

Syntax:

=IF(logical_Test, Value_if_true,Value_if_False)

- logical_Test: This is the condition for the present scenario.
- Value_if_true: This is the value or calculation to be shown if logical_Test is True.
- Value_if_False: This is vthe value or calculation to be shown if logical_Test is False.

Let's consider a suitable example. Below is a list of students and their scores. Let's assume that the passing marks are 33. So the condition is that if a student score is greater than or equal to 33, then that student has passed else he/she has failed. See the following *Figure 4.24*:

	A	B	C
1		Student Score Card	
2	Student	Score	Pass/Fail
3	Student 1	40	
4	Student 2	13	
5	Student 3	95	
6	Student 4	16	
7	Student 5	79	
8	Student 6	36	
9	Student 7	66	
10	Student 8	73	
11	Student 9	58	
12	Student 10	14	
13			
14	*Passing Marks: 33*		

Figure 4.24

Apply the IF function for the first student (see the following *Figure 4.25*) then just copy and paste it for the rest of the students:

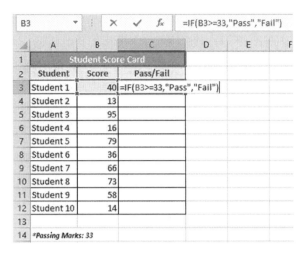

Figure 4.25

IFS

Note: This has already been discussed under "New functions" in Chapter 1.

AND

You can use this function when you want to check if all the conditions are True.

Syntax:

AND(logical1, [logical2], …)

The arguments are as follows:

- logical1: This is the required argument. This is the first condition to be evaluated (it could either be TRUE or FALSE).

- logical2: This is the optional argument. These are additional conditions to be evaluated to either TRUE or FALSE; there can be up to a maximum of 255 conditions.

Suppose, you want to evaluate the scores of multiple students for multiple subjects. The condition is that if a student scores 33 or more in all the subjects, only then he/ she will be considered to have passes else the student has failed. See the following *Figure 4.26*:

▲	A	B	C	D	E	F
1	Student Score Card					
2	Student	Sbject 1	Sbject 2	Sbject 3	Pass/Fail	
3	Student 1	48	31	54		
4	Student 2	39	19	24		
5	Student 3	61	51	78		
6	Student 4	47	71	77		
7	Student 5	60	11	17		
8	Student 6	42	25	42		
9	Student 7	56	18	66		
10	Student 8	30	69	76		
11	Student 9	79	21	63		
12	Student 10	33	56	52		
13						
14	*Passing Marks: 33*					

Figure 4.26

Using the AND function alone will give the result either True or False, but if we nest IF and AND, we can have our desired result as Pass or Fail. Just to keep things simple, let's first use the AND function alone. See the following *Figure 4.27*:

▲	A	B	C	D	E	F	G
1	Student Score Card						
2	Student	Sbject 1	Sbject 2	Sbject 3	Pass/Fail		
3	Student 1	48	31	54	=AND(B3>=33,C3>=33,D3>=33)		
4	Student 2	39	19	24			
5	Student 3	61	51	78			
6	Student 4	47	71	77			
7	Student 5	60	11	17			
8	Student 6	42	25	42			
9	Student 7	56	18	66			
10	Student 8	30	69	76			
11	Student 9	79	21	63			
12	Student 10	33	56	52			
13							
14	*Passing Marks: 33*						

Figure 4.27

OR

The OR function will give the result true if any one out of a set of conditions is True.

Syntax:

OR(logical1, [logical2], ...)

The arguments are explained as follows:

- logical1: This is the required argument. This is the first condition that you want to evaluate to be either TRUE or FALSE.

- logical2: This is the optional argument. These are additional conditions that you want to evaluate to be either TRUE or FALSE. There can be up to a maximum of 255 conditions.

Let's assume that now a student will be considered as "Pass" if he/she gets 33 or more in any one of the subjects.

The OR function will look similar to an AND function. See the following *Figure 4.28*:

SUM		X ✓ *fx*		=OR(B3>=33,C3>=33,D3>=33)		
	A	B	C	D	E	F	G
1		Student Score Card					
2	Student	Sbject 1	Sbject 2	Sbject 3	Pass/Fail		
3	Student 1	48	31	54	=OR(B3>=33,C3>=33,D3>=33)		
4	Student 2	39	19	24			
5	Student 3	61	51	78			
6	Student 4	47	71	77			
7	Student 5	60	11	17			
8	Student 6	42	25	42			
9	Student 7	56	18	66			
10	Student 8	30	69	76			
11	Student 9	79	21	63			
12	Student 10	33	56	52			
13							
14	*Passing Marks: 33*						C

Figure 4.28

NOT

The NOT function simply returns the opposite of the given logical condition.

Syntax:

=NOT (logical)

The arguments are as follows:

- logical: It is a value or logical expression that can be evaluated as TRUE or FALSE.

Consider the same example we used to discuss the IF function, but this time let's reverse it using the NOT function. The actual condition is to check whether the value is greater than or equal to 33 or not, but the NOT function will reverse the outcome (which is a bit illogical, but this is just to understand the function). The function will look as shown in the following *Figure 4.29*:

▲	A	B	C
1	Student Score Card		
2	Student	Score	Pass/Fail
3	Student 1	40	=NOT(B3>=33)
4	Student 2	13	
5	Student 3	95	
6	Student 4	16	
7	Student 5	79	
8	Student 6	36	
9	Student 7	66	
10	Student 8	73	
11	Student 9	58	
12	Student 10	14	
13			
14	*Passing Marks: 33		

Figure 4.29

Text functions

Excel is not a **Data Base Management System** (**DBMS**) that is; it is only used to analyze data that is extracted from other source. As a result, the extracted data isn't always in the desired form. It needs to be cleaned first, and that is where these Text functions come into play. Let's understand their practical use one by one.

Exercise file

A workbook containing the exercise files used in this chapter for Text functions in Excel, is available on https://rebrand.ly/ffdbc, the file is named 4.5 Text Functions. xlsx. You can download it and practice along.

UPPER, LOWER, and PROPER

The following three functions help in converting unsymmetrical text into symmetrical one.

UPPER: It will convert the text into upper-case.

Syntax:

UPPER(text)

- text: This is the required argument. This is the text you want converted to uppercase. It can be a reference or text string.

LOWER: It will convert the text into lower-case.

Syntax:

LOWER(text)

- text: This is the required argument. The-is is the text you want to convert to lowercase. It does not change characters that are not letters.

PROPER: It will capitalize the first character of the text and change the rest of the characters to lower case. It will repeat this after each blank space.

Syntax:

PROPER(text)

- text: This is the required argument. This includes text enclosed in quotation marks, a formula that returns text, or a reference to a cell containing the text you want to partially capitalize.

Let's take a sample data set of customer names written in jumbled cases. See the following *Figure 4.30*:

	A	B	C	D
1	Customer Data			
2	First Name	Upper	Lower	Proper
3	ArJUn			
4	DeePAk			
5	anUJ			
6	sunil			
7	allA			
8	MUKESh			
9				

Figure 4.30

You can use the three functions as shown in the following *Figure 4.31*:

▲	A	B	C	D
1	**Customer Data**			
2	**First Name**	**Upper**	**Lower**	**Proper**
3	ArJUn	=UPPER(A3)	=LOWER(A3)	=PROPER(A3)
4	DeePAk			
5	anUJ			
6	sunil			
7	allA			
8	MUKESh			
9				

Figure 4.31

LEFT, RIGHT, and MID

These functions help in fetching characters from left, right, or middle of the content of a cell. These are commonly used for symmetrical data such as employee ID, SSN number, and vehicle number that comprise of a fixed number of characters. Important data can be extracted using these functions.

LEFT: This function is used to fetch characters from the left side of the cell as per the number of characters you specify.

Syntax:

LEFT (text, [num_chars])

- text: This is the required argument. This is the text string that contains the characters you want to extract.

- num_chars: This is the optional argument. This is used to specify the number of characters you want to extract from the left side of the cell.

- num_chars must be greater than or equal to zero.

- If num_chars is greater than the length of text, LEFT returns all of the text.

- If num_chars is omitted, it is assumed to be 1.

RIGHT: This function is used to fetch characters from the right side of the cell as per the number of characters you specify.

Syntax:

RIGHT(text,[num_chars])

- text: This is the required argument. This is the text string containing the characters you want to extract.

- num_chars: This is the optional argument. This specifies the number of characters you want to extract from the right side of the cell.

MID: Use this function to fetch characters starting from the character you specify and the number of characters you specify.

Syntax:

MID(text, start_num, num_chars)

- text: This is the required argument. This is the text string containing the characters you want to extract.

- start_num: This is the required argument. This is the position of the first character you want to extract. The first character in text is start_num 1 and so on.

- num_chars: This is the required argument. This specifies the number of characters you want to extract from the middle of the cell.

Below is a list of product IDs, which is a combination of Product, State and Invoice Number. Let's use the above functions to extract specific parts of text from the Product ID. See the following *Figure 4.32*:

	A	B	C	D
1			Products	
2	Product ID	Product	State	Invoice Number
3	FUR-BO-10001798			
4	FUR-CH-10000454			
5	OFF-LA-10000240			
6	FUR-TA-10000577			
7	OFF-ST-10000760			
8	FUR-FU-10001487			
9	OFF-AR-10002833			
10	TEC-PH-10002275			
11				

Figure 4.32

As you can see in the preceding figure, the first three characters of the product ID represent the product type, following two characters represent the State code, and the last eight characters represent the Invoice Number. Now let's fetch them each group of characters using these functions. See the following *Figure 4.33*:

	A	B	C	D
1		Products		
2	Product ID	Product	State	Invoice Number
3	FUR-BO-10001798	=LEFT(A3,3)	=MID(A3,5,2)	=RIGHT(A3,8)
4	FUR-CH-10000454			
5	OFF-LA-10000240			
6	FUR-TA-10000577			
7	OFF-ST-10000760			
8	FUR-FU-10001487			
9	OFF-AR-10002833			
10	TEC-PH-10002275			
11				

Figure 4.33

CONCATENATE, "&"

Concatenate is used to join content/cells, whereas "&" is just a substitute of CONCATENATE.

Syntax:

CONCATENATE(text1, [text2], …)

- text1: This is the required argument. This is the first item to join. The item can be a text value, number, or cell reference.

- text2: This is the optional argument. Additional text items to join. You can have up to 255 items, up to a total of 8,192 characters.

Consider the previous example again. Now suppose the product type, state code, and invoice number are given separately and you want to join them (with hyphens as shown in the figure) to create a product ID. That's where you can use the CONCATENATE function. See the following *Figure 4.34*:

	A	B	C	D	E
1			Products		
2	Product	State	Invoice Number	Product ID	Product ID
3	FUR	BO	10001798		
4	FUR	CH	10000454		
5	OFF	LA	10000240		
6	FUR	TA	10000577		
7	OFF	ST	10000760		
8	FUR	FU	10001487		
9	OFF	AR	10002833		
10	TEC	PH	10002275		
11					

Figure 4.34

You can use either CONCATENATE or & to create a product ID. See the following *Figure 4.35*:

	A	B	C	D	E
1			Products		
2	Product	State	Invoice Number	Product ID	Product ID
3	FUR	BO	10001798	=CONCATENATE(A3,"-",B3,"-",C3)	=A3&"-"&B3&"-"&C3
4	FUR	CH	10000454		
5	OFF	LA	10000240		
6	FUR	TA	10000577		
7	OFF	ST	10000760		
8	FUR	FU	10001487		
9	OFF	AR	10002833		
10	TEC	PH	10002275		
11					

Figure 4.35

TRIM

It is quite common to end up having data with unwanted spaces. As the name suggests, the TRIM function simply trims them out.

Syntax:

TRIM(text)

- text: This is the required argument. This is the text from which you want spaces removed.

Below is a sample database of names of various software with some unwanted spaces (although not visible here). See the following *Figure 4.36*:

	A	B
1	Initial Database	Trimmed Data
2	200684165 MQPML ATF MQ SPECIAL EVENTS FD Internal $10,065.49 CR	
3	201853058 MBL-MGI REPS TXN A/C Internal $0.00 CR	
4	202352225 NINE 2002 - TRUST A/C Internal $117,927.20 CR	
5	202649638 TXN - RFX NOV 06 Internal $1,558.09 CR	
6	206423089 ALMONDS 2007 - TXN A/C Internal $6,940.06 CR	
7	208743393 MAC EQUINOX - TRUST ACCOUNT Internal $88.00 CR	
8	211924246 TIMBER LAND TRUST 2007 Internal $43,617.12 CR	
9	212169635 NINE 2003 - TXN A/C Internal $0.00 CR	
10	213477359 TRUST - RFX COMMODITY Internal $565,936.93 CR	
11	214177453 FORESTRY 2008 - LAND S1017E Internal $0.00 CR	
12	214422560 TXN - CIR MAR 08 Internal $3,000.00 CR	
13	214430316 MQ MAC EQ ASIA 2 Internal $96.96 CR	
14	216335778 MFPML ATF RGV SOPH INV TRUST Internal $25,931.81 DR	
15	221114481 MDAF - TXN A/C Internal $47,366.62 CR	

Figure 4.36

Use the TRIM function to remove these spaces, as shown in *Figure 4.37*:

	A	B
1	**Initial Database**	**Trimmed Data**
2	200684165 MQPML ATF MQ SPECIAL EVENTS FD Internal $10,065.49 CR	=TRIM(A2)
3	201853058 MBL-MGI REPS TXN A/C Internal $0.00 CR	
4	202352225 NINE 2002 - TRUST A/C Internal $117,927.20 CR	
5	202649638 TXN - RFX NOV 06 Internal $1,558.09 CR	
6	206423089 ALMONDS 2007 - TXN A/C Internal $6,940.06 CR	
7	208743393 MAC EQUINOX - TRUST ACCOUNT Internal $88.00 CR	
8	211924246 TIMBER LAND TRUST 2007 Internal $43,617.12 CR	
9	212169635 NINE 2003 - TXN A/C Internal $0.00 CR	
10	213477359 TRUST - RFX COMMODITY Internal $565,936.93 CR	
11	214177453 FORESTRY 2008 - LAND S1017E Internal $0.00 CR	
12	214422560 TXN - CIR MAR 08 Internal $3,000.00 CR	
13	214430316 MQ MAC EQ ASIA 2 Internal $96.96 CR	
14	216335778 MFPML ATF RGV SOPH INV TRUST Internal $25,931.81 DR	
15	221114481 MDAF - TXN A/C Internal $47,366.62 CR	
16		

Figure 4.37

FIND, and SEARCH

These functions help in finding a character or a text string present in a cell. If a character or text string appears multiple times in the cell, you can define the position from where you want to find/.

FIND: This function helps in finding a character or text string present in a cell, and it is case sensitive.

Syntax:

FIND(find_text, within_text, [start_num])

- find_text: This is the required argument. This is the text you want to find.

- within_text: This is the required argument. This is the text containing the text you want to find.

- start_num: This is the optional argument. This specifies the character at which to start the search. The first character in within_text is character number 1. If you omit start_num, it is assumed to be 1.

SEARCH: This function also helps in finding a character or text string present in a cell, but it is not case sensitive.

Syntax:

SEARCH(find_text, within_text, [start_num])

- find_text: This is the required argument. This is the text you want to find.

- within_text: This is the required argument. This is the text containing the text you want to find.

- start_num: This is the optional argument. This specifies the character at which to start the search. The first character in within_text is character number 1. If you omit start_num, it is assumed to be 1.

Here is a list of student names with a space in between their first and last names. Thus, we can separate their first and last name by finding the position of the space. Let's see how the FIND/SEARCH function works if we use it to find the position of the space. See the following *Figure 4.38*:

	A	B
1	Student Data	
2	Student Name	Space
3	Manshi Sharma	
4	Simran Kumari	
5	Bijan Gope	
6	Sunanda Das	
7	Raj Kumar Sinha	
8	Shivani Chaturvedi	
9	Abilash Das	

Figure 4.38

The FIND function will look as show in *Figure 4.39*):

	A	B
1	Student Data	
2	Student Name	Space
3	Manshi Sharma	=FIND(" ",A3)
4	Simran Kumari	
5	Bijan Gope	
6	Sunanda Das	
7	Raj Kumar Sinha	
8	Shivani Chaturvedi	
9	Abilash Das	

Figure 4.39

The outcome of this function will be "7," because the space appears at the 7th position in cell A3. SEARCH function can also be used in the same manner.

Date & Time functions

When it comes to working with date and time, these functions are a real time-saver. Excel offers a bucket of these functions, and they help in not only formatting the given date and time but also to calculate minutes, hours, days, weeks, months, years, etc., on the basis of the present or past data. Just keep in mind that dates and or time in Excel are actually stored as sequential serial numbers, and that is why all these functions are able to calculate. Let's discuss some of the most commonly used date and time functions.

Exercise file

A workbook containing the exercise files used in this chapter for Date & Time functions in Excel, is available on https://rebrand.ly/ffdbc, the file is named 4.6 Date & Time Functions.xlsx. You can download it and practice along.

DAY, MONTH, YEAR

These functions help in finding the serial number of the respective period from a given date.

DAY: This function will find the serial number of the day out from a given date.

Syntax:

DAY(serial_number)

- serial_number: This is the required argument. This is the date for the day you are trying to find.

MONTH: This function will find the serial number of the month from a given date.

Syntax

MONTH(serial_number)

- serial_number: This is the required argument. This is the date for the month you are trying to find.

YEAR: This function will find the serial number of the year from a given date.

Syntax:

YEAR(serial_number)

- serial_number: This is the required argument. This is the date for the year you are trying to find.

suppose the given date is 18-02-2019. The outcome of the three will be as shown in the following *Figure 4.40*:

◢	A	B	C	D	E	F
1		Date				
2		18-02-2019		Day	18	=DAY(B2)
3						
4				Month	2	=MONTH(B2)
5						
6				Year	2019	=YEAR(B2)
7						

Figure 4.40

TODAY and NOW

These functions will show today's system (computer) date and time. The outcome is dynamic, that is, it changes as and when we perform any action like entering data or opening or closing a workbook or worksheet. For example, you apply these functions today and then open Excel tomorrow, then the outcome will automatically get changed to tomorrow's date.

TODAY: This function will show the current system date as the outcome.

Syntax:

TODAY()

This function's syntax has no arguments.

NOW: This function will show the current system date and time as the outcome.

Syntax:

NOW()

This function's syntax too has no arguments.

We can use these functions in isolation (see the following *Figure 4.41*) or nest them with other functions. For example, to update the age of a person, you can use his/her birth date and then apply the TODAY function. This way Excel will keep on showing you the updated age:

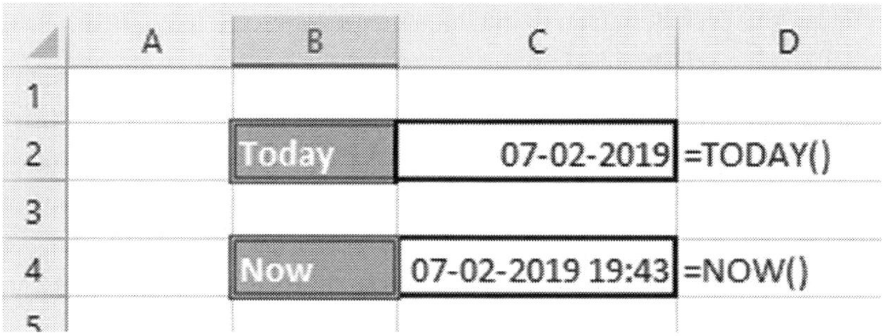

Figure 4.41

EDATE

This function will show us a serial number or a date that is the indicated number of months before or after a specified date. We generally use it to calculate due dates.

Syntax:

EDATE(start_date, months)

- start_date: This is the required argument. This is a date that represents the start date.

- months: This is the required argument. This is the number of months before or after start_date. A positive value for months yields a future date; a negative value yields a past date.

Let's understand the same with two different examples. We'll use the same date for both the examples, but in one case we will set the number of months as +6 (future) and in the other case we will set it as -3 (past). See the following *Figure 4.42*:

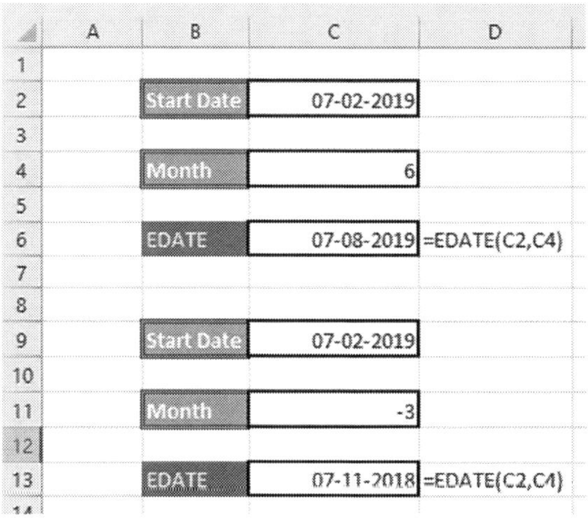

Figure 4.42

EOMONTH

EOMONTH stands for End Of Month. It returns the serial number for the last day of the month that is the indicated number of months before or after the start date. It is generally used to calculate due dates.

Syntax:

EOMONTH(start_date, months)

- start_date: This is the required argument. This is a date that represents the starting date.

- months: This is the required argument. This is the number of months before or after start_date. A positive value for months yields a future date; a negative value yields a past date.

Let's assume that we have signed an annual maintenance contract on a particular day for a product for 12 months. We can find out due date of this AMC using the EOMONTH function. See the following *Figure 4.43*:

	A	B	C	D
1				
2		AMC Start Date	31-01-2019	
3				
4		Month	12	
5				
6		EOMonth	31-01-2020	=EOMONTH(C2,C4)
7				

Figure 4.43

NETWORKDAYS and NETWORKDAYS.INTL

These functions are useful when you used to find the total number of working days between two dates. The only difference between these two is that NETWORKDAYS will consider Saturday and Sunday as weekly off by default, whereas in the case of NETWORKDAYS.INTL function weekend can be selected from a given set of options.

NETWORKDAYS

This function returns the number of working days between a start date and an end date, excluding Saturday and Sunday.

Syntax:

NETWORKDAYS(start_date, end_date, [holidays])

- start_date: This is the required argument. This is a date that represents the start date.

- end_date: This is the required argument. This is a date that represents the end date.

- holidays: This is the optional argument. This is an optional range of one or more dates to exclude from the working calendar.

NETWORKDAYS.INTL

This function returns the number of working days between a start date and an end date excluding a specified weekend.

Syntax:

NETWORKDAYS.INTL(start_date, end_date, [weekend], [holidays])

- start_date, end_date: This is the required argument. These are the dates for which the difference is to be computed. The start_date can be earlier than, the same as, or later than the end_date.

- weekend: This is the optional argument. This indicates the days of the week that are weekend days and are not included in the number of whole working days between start_date and end_date. Weekend is a weekend number or string that specifies when weekends occur.

The following table (*Table No. 4.1*) shows weekend number values corresponding to different weekend days:

Weekend number	Weekend days
1 or omitted	Saturday, Sunday
2	Sunday, Monday
3	Monday, Tuesday
4	Tuesday, Wednesday
5	Wednesday, Thursday
6	Thursday, Friday
7	Friday, Saturday
11	Sunday only
12	Monday only

Weekend number	Weekend days
13	Tuesday only
14	Wednesday only
15	Thursday only
16	Friday only
17	Saturday only

Weekend string values are seven characters long, and each character in the string represents a day of the week, starting with Monday. 1 represents a non-workday and 0 represents a workday. Only the characters 1 and 0 are permitted in the string. Using 1111111 will always return 0.

For example, 0000011 would result in a weekend that is Saturday and Sunday.

Holidays (optional). This is an optional set of one or more dates that are to be excluded from the working day calendar. holidays shall be a range of cells that contain the dates or an array constant of the serial values that represent those dates. The ordering of dates or serial values in holidays can be arbitrary.

Let's consider the following example where we have a list of holidays with a start and an end date. We will use both functions to calculate the total number of working days. See the following *Figure 4.44*:

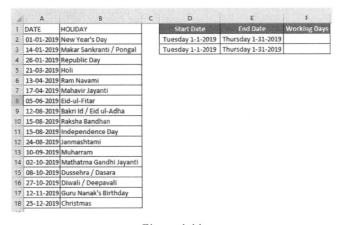

Figure 4.44

For NETWORKDAYS, weekend is Saturday and Sunday both, but for NETWORKDAYS. INTL weekend is only Sunday. That's why we get different outcomes for the number of working days in January 2019. See the following *Figure 4.45*:

D	E	F	G	H	I	J	K
Start Date	**End Date**	**Working Days**					
Tuesday 1-1-2019	Thursday 1-31-2019	21	=NETWORKDAYS(D2,E2,A2:A18)	<== Saturday and Sunday as weekend			
Tuesday 1-1-2019	Thursday 1-31-2019	24	=NETWORKDAYS.INTL(D3,E3,11,A2:A18)	<== Only Sunday as weeekend			

Figure 4.45

Lookup functions

Lookup functionality is one of the most commonly used buckets of functions. These functions are used to fetch details of columns corresponding to common columns. It's also very useful in comparing two sets of data. For example, if we have similar data for two different customers in a database, we can use these functions to update the data accordingly. Let's consider some real-life, practical examples to understand these functions. But before we do so, first we need to understand how to freeze a cell reference, that is, the use of $ sign, because this will play a vital role in using these functions.

Exercise file

A workbook containing the exercise files used in this chapter for Lookup functionality in Excel, is available on https://rebrand.ly/ffdbc, the file is named 4.7 Lookup Functionality.xlsx. You can download it and practice along.

Understanding references and use of $ sign

Let's understand some most important types of cell reference and the use of $ sign one by one.

Relative reference: Whenever we copy a cell reference and paste it in another cell the cell content will change accordingly. Excel by default works on this reference. This is actually the strength of Excel; it is because of only this feature that you need to apply a function or a formula only once, and thereafter, you can just copy and paste it throughout, to get the results for all. In *Figure 4.46* below, let's find the profit for each sales transaction. You can simply subtract the purchase amount from the sales amount. But you will get profit/loss for the rest of the transactions only if the cell reference changes for all the cells:

	D4	▾	:	×	✓	*fx*	=E4-D4		

▲	A	B	C	D	E	F
1			**Relative Reference**			
2						
3	Product	Category	Department	Purchase Price	Sale Price	Profit/Loss
4	Dry Tissues	Cleaning Supplies	Household	120	135	=E4-D4
5	Paper Towels	Cleaning Supplies	Household	125	135	
6	Wet Wipes	Cleaning Supplies	Household	120	135	
7	Chicken Dinner	Frozen Foods	Grocery	80	155	
8	Clear Refresher	Soft Drinks	Grocery	165	100	
9	Dried Grits	Salty Snacks	Grocery	180	100	
10	Extra Nougat	Candy	Grocery	145	115	

Figure 4.46

Just copy and paste the function of cell F4 below, and you can have all the solutions.

Absolute reference: This reference is an opposite of relative reference. Sometimes in a calculation, we would like to freeze a certain cell reference. For this, we use the $ sign as a symbol before and after the cell reference. Let's take an example where a fixed tax rate and different unit prices are given. You want to calculate the tax for each product unit by multiplying the fixed tax rate (given in a cell) by each unit price (given in multiple cells). Without the use of $ sign, you will have to apply the same calculation for all the unit prices individually But by using the $ sign before and after the cell reference, i.e., column H and row 3, you can freeze the tax rate completely. See the following *Figure 4.47* to understand how to freeze a cell reference using the $ sign:

=G5*$H$3						

C	D	E	F	G	H	I
		Absolute Reference				
					5%	
Customer	Quantity	Category	Code	Unit Price	GST	Amount
Jindol Sinha	5	Suits	W1	3200	=G5*$H$3	3360.00
Dola Das	3	Coats	H2	1250		1250.00
Deepak Sharma	4	Coats	C4	1250		1250.00
Uma Nag	12	Ties	T1	150		150.00
Sayak Pal	6	Hats	C1	99		99.00
Srijan Das	10	Suits	W1	3200		3200.00

Figure 4.47

Mixed Reference: Using $ either before a column or row is known as mixed reference. Sometimes it becomes important to take reference from both column and row, out of which either of them needs to freeze. Given below is a list of sales persons and their target sales amount, along with the target percentage they are supposed to achieve every month for the next 6 months. If we don't use mixed reference here then it would be difficult to get the correct result. Let's see how we can apply the same. See the following *Figure 4.48*:

	A	B	C	D	E	F	G	H
1			Mixed Reference					
2								
3			6 Months Sales Target					
4	Sales Person	Target (in	12%	8%	15%	25%	22%	18%
5		INR)	January	February	March	April	May	June
6	Jinia Ghosh	164506	=$B6*C$4					
7	Alok Kundu	186343						
8	Soham Das	155543						
9	Sandip Jana	101719						
10	Nilay Guha	192612						
11	Mrinal Kayal	198205						

Figure 4.48

VLOOKUP

VLOOKUP function is used to look up values on a vertical table array.

Syntax:

VLOOKUP (lookup_value, table_array, col_index_num, [range_lookup])

- lookup_value: This is the required argument. This is the value you want to look up. The value you want to look up must be in the first column of the range of cells you specify in table-array.

- table_array: This is the required argument. This is the range of cells in which the VLOOKUP will search for the lookup_value and the return value.

- col_index_num: This is the required argument. This is the column number (starting with 1 for the left-most column of table-array) that contains the return value.

- range_lookup: This is the optional argument. This is a logical value that specifies whether you want VLOOKUP to find an approximate or an exact match:

If TRUE then the first column in the table is sorted either numerically or alphabetically, and VLOOKUP will then search for the closest value. This is the default method if you don't specify one.

If FALSE then VLOOKUP searches for the exact value in the first column.

VLOOKUP False case: Let's first understand how VLOOKUP works for an exact match.

On the left side of *Figure 4.49* below are invoices for different products. However, their prices are missing. On the right side of the sheet we have products and their prices. Now let's use the VLOOKUP function to fetch the price from the product and price table to our invoices table. Because a product name is unique and it is exactly available in both the tables, it is considered as lookup_value. The table on the right, from where we will fetch the price, will be our *Table array* (we will freeze it as *absolute reference* too. Because we need to take the values from the second column, that is, Price so col_Index_num will be 2. And finally, as mentioned previously, as the lookup value (product name) is an exact match in both the tables, range_lookup will either be False or 0. See the following *Figure 4.49*:

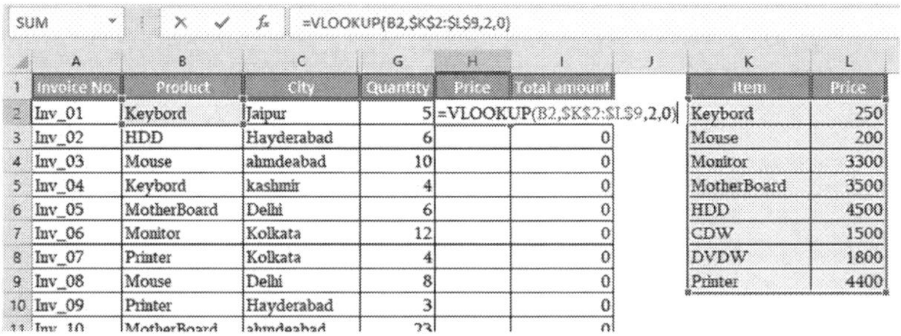

SUM | =VLOOKUP(B2,$K$2:$L$9,2,0)

	A	B	C	G	H	I	J	K	L
1	Invoice No.	Product	City	Quantity	Price	Total amount		Item	Price
2	Inv_01	Keybord	Jaipur	5	=VLOOKUP(B2,$K$2:$L$9,2,0)			Keybord	250
3	Inv_02	HDD	Hayderabad	6		0		Mouse	200
4	Inv_03	Mouse	ahmdeabad	10		0		Monitor	3300
5	Inv_04	Keybord	kashmir	4		0		MotherBoard	3500
6	Inv_05	MotherBoard	Delhi	6		0		HDD	4500
7	Inv_06	Monitor	Kolkata	12		0		CDW	1500
8	Inv_07	Printer	Kolkata	4		0		DVDW	1800
9	Inv_08	Mouse	Delhi	8		0		Printer	4400
10	Inv_09	Printer	Hayderabad	3		0			
11	Inv_10	MotherBoard	ahmdeabad	23		0			

Figure 4.49

VLOOKUP True case: When range_lookup is set to True, VLOOKUP will try to find an approximate match. Let's understand the same with a sample data set. Below is a list of products and their prices. On the right side of the sheet is another table containing the price slab and discount (%). The discount increases with the price. Here lookup_value will be the price on the left-hand side table. table_array is the right side table. col_index_num" is 2 because discount (%) is in the second column of table_array and range_lookup will be either True or 1 as prices are not unique and are given in the form of numerals in table_array. See the following *Figure 4.50*:

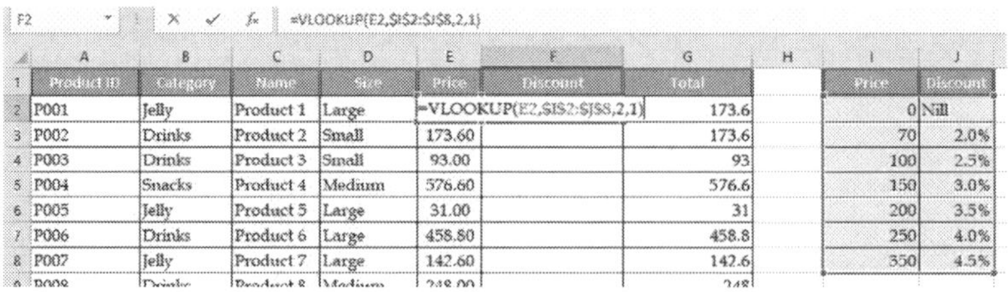

F2 | =VLOOKUP(E2,$I$2:$J$8,2,1)

	A	B	C	D	E	F	G	H	I	J
1	Product ID	Category	Name	Size	Price	Discount	Total		Price	Discount
2	P001	Jelly	Product 1	Large	=VLOOKUP(E2,$I$2:$J$8,2,1)		173.6		0	Nill
3	P002	Drinks	Product 2	Small	173.60		173.6		70	2.0%
4	P003	Drinks	Product 3	Small	93.00		93		100	2.5%
5	P004	Snacks	Product 4	Medium	576.60		576.6		150	3.0%
6	P005	Jelly	Product 5	Large	31.00		31		200	3.5%
7	P006	Drinks	Product 6	Large	458.80		458.8		250	4.0%
8	P007	Jelly	Product 7	Large	142.60		142.6		350	4.5%
9	P008	Drinks	Product 8	Medium	248.00		248			

Figure 4.50

HLOOKUP

This function works exactly like VLOOKUP except it works horizontally rather than vertically.

Syntax:

HLOOKUP(lookup_value, table_array, row_index_num, [range_lookup])

- lookup_value: This is the required argument. This is the value to be found in the first row of the table. lookup_value can be a value, reference, or text string.

- table_array: This is the required argument. This is the table from which data is looked up. Use a reference to a range or a range name. The values in the first row of table_array can be text, numbers, or logical values.

- row_index_num: This is the required argument. This is the row number in table_array from which the matching value will be returned. A row_index_num of 1 returns the first row value in table_array, row_index_num of 2 returns the second row value in table_array, and so on.

- range_lookup: This is the optional argument. It is a logical value that specifies whether you want HLOOKUP to find an exact match or an approximate match. If TRUE or omitted, an approximate match is returned.

HLOOKUP False case: In the example shown below (*Figure 4.51*), month-wise sales data is shown for each sales representative. Let's fetch the sales amount for one of the sales representatives and for a particular month. Here, lookup_value will be the name of that sales representative. table_array will the horizontally placed sales data at the top of the sheet. row_index_num will be the row number of the month for which we are looking up and finally range_lookup will be false or 0 as names are unique in this data set:

	A	B	C	D	E	F	G	H	I	J	K
	Sales Rep.	Bikash Singh	Sanjoy Kumar	Rishik Sen	Surajit das	Ajit Roy	Robert Peter	Rahul Singh	Debasish Dey	Manoj Patra	Supriyo Neogi	Bijay Sharma
2	April	45012	201532	20485	35960	312500	452013	48500	654186	604520	874215
3	May	48520	452147	86158	589721	203654	75014	304520	94201	50423	58875
4	June	500142	565248	50365	83015	795421	520452	85690	48759	684215	970145
5	July	847521	304258	387451	95230	542874	61820	87125	230458	632145	853710
6	August	856314	258961	204582	795612	304692	30485	75920	504287	30125	95871
7	September	697458	61201	52485	623458	945301	96312	485230	487560	60450	84521
8											
9											
10	Sales Rep.	June									
11	Manoj Patra	=HLOOKUP(A11,A1:K7,4,0)									

Figure 4.51

HLOOKUP True case: To understand this consider the same example sales representatives with their sales amount mentioned. Now let's assign a respective commission rate based on the table given on the right side of the sheet. Here, lookup_value will be the sales amount of each representative. table_array will be the commission rate table on the right side of the sheet. row_index_num will be 2 because commission rate is mentioned in the second row of table_array. range_lookup will be True or 1 as sales values are not unique. See the following *Figure 4.52*:

D2		×	✓	*fx*	=HLOOKUP(C2,$G$1:$M$2,2,1)								
	A	B	C	D	E	F	G	H	I	J	K	L	M
1	Date	Sales Rep	Sales	Commission		Sales	0	100	500	1000	2500	5000	9000
2	01-03-2016	Rhonda	4190.46	=HLOOKUP(C2,$G$1:$M$2,2,1)			Nill	2%	4%	5%	7%	9%	10%
3	03-08-2014	Luke	3462.65										
4	24-05-2015	Steven	8687.12										

Figure 4.52

LOOKUP

The advantage of using LOOKUP is that it can look up values vertically as well as horizontally. Also, it can look up in any direction of the data unlike VLOOKUP that can look up only towards right or HLOOKUP that can look up only downwards. The only disadvantage of LOOKUP (that cannot be ignored) is that it can only work for an approximate match.

Syntax:

LOOKUP(lookup_value, lookup_vector, [result_vector])

- lookup_value: This is the required argument. This is a value that LOOKUP searches for in the first vector. lookup_value can be a number, text, a logical value, or a name or reference that refers to a value.

- lookup_vector: This is the required argument. This is a range that contains only one row or one column. The values in lookup_vector can be text, numbers, or logical values.

- result_vector: This is the optional argument. This is a range that contains only one row or column. The result_vector argument must be the same size as lookup_vector.

Let's take the same sample data set we used to understand the *Vlookup True case* but with a small change; table_array lookup values are on the right and resulting cells are on the left (which VLOOKUP cannot fetch). Here, lookup_value is same as before, price. lookup_vector the price range given in the table on the right, and result_vector will be the discount (%) in the table. See the following *Figure 4.53*:

C	D	E	F	G	H	I	J
=LOOKUP(E2,$J$2:$J$8,$I$2:$I$8)							
ame	Size	Price	Discount	Total		Discount	Price
luct 1	Large	173.60	=LOOKUP(E2,$J$2:$J$8,$I$2:$I$8)	173.57		Nill	0
luct 2	Small	173.60		173.6		2.0%	70
luct 3	Small	93.00		93		2.5%	100
luct 4	Medium	576.60		576.6		3.0%	150
luct 5	Large	31.00		31		3.5%	200
luct 6	Large	458.80		458.8		4.0%	250
luct 7	Large	142.60		142.6		4.5%	350

Figure 4.53

INDEX and MATCH

Any limitations in the previous Lookup functions are overcome using the INDEX and MATCH functions, as this combinations can look up in any direction and can work for an exact match too.

MATCH: This function helps in finding the position of a value in a range.

Syntax:

MATCH(lookup_value, lookup_array, [match_type])

- lookup_value: This is the required argument. This is the value that you want to match in lookup_array. It can be a value (number, text, or logical value) or a cell reference to a number, text, or logical value.

- lookup_array: This is the required argument. This is the range of cells being searched.

- match_type: This is the optional argument. This is a number whose value can be -1, 0, or 1. The match_type argument specifies how Excel matches lookup_value with values in lookup_array. The default value for this argument is 1.

INDEX: This function can fetch values across a table for a given row and column number.

Syntax:

INDEX(array, row_num, [column_num])

- array: This is the required argument. This is a range of cells or an array constant. If array contains only one row or column, the corresponding row_num or column_num argument is optional. If array has more than one row and column, and only row_num or column_num is used, INDEX returns an array of the entire row or column in array.

- row_num: This is the required argument. This selects the row in array from which to return a value. If row_num is omitted, column_num is required.

- column_num: This is the optional argument. This selects the column in array from which to return a value. If column_num is omitted, row_num is required.

Let's consider the example of a bank's database. It contains account numbers and the respective balance available in each account type, that is, Current, Savings, Recurring, or FD. Let's find the balance amount for a given Account Number and a given Account Type. As it's a two-way lookup, we will nest the MATCH function inside the INDEX function to get the desired result. Let's start with the INDEX function, where array will be the complete table. For row_num (as it contains a dropdown list of all the account numbers) we will apply the MATCH function, where lookup_value will be the account number currently selected from the drop-down list. lookup_array will be column A that has all the account numbers, and match_type will be False or 0. For col_num argument of the Index function we will again use the MATCH function, because it is again a drop-down list of all the account types and you can change it anytime. lookup_value will be the account type that is currently selected from the dropdown list. lookup_array will be the headers, data and match type will be either exact match or 0. See the following *Figure 4.54*:

Figure 4.54

Summary

Formulas and functions play a vital role in Excel. In this chapter, we have discussed the most commonly used basic to advanced Excel functions. We have gone through the syntax and arguments of each function. We have covered only a handful of functions in this book; there are over 200 functions available in Excel and this number is only increasing with each new version. If you would like to explore more them, you can also use the **Help** menu (shortcut *F1* key).

Now that we have understood the logic behind function/formula writing, next chapter is dedicated to data analysis, where you will learn to use Excel's most amazing tools such as pivot table, What-if analysis, and power tools.

CHAPTER 5

Data Analysis

Data analysis is the process of using tools that help in understanding the transformed data, which ultimately helps in decision-making. Excel not only provides tools to clean up the data but also helps in analyzing the data sets in a very easy manner. It offers tools such as Pivot Tables, What-If analysis, and Solver, along with Power BI tools like Power Pivot and Power Query. In this chapter, we will understand how, when, and where to use these powerful tools.

Structure:

In this chapter, we will discuss:

- Pivot tables
- Calculation and grouping options in pivot table
- Power Query
- Power Pivot
- What-If analysis
- Solver
- Analysis ToolPak
- Forecast sheet

Objective

After reading this chapter, you will be able to use the amazing data analysis tools in Excel to analyze your data more efficiently and effectively. This chapter will explain data cleansing techniques to help you extract meaningful information from the data, based on which decisions can be made.

Pivot tables

Pivot table is one of the most popular tools used to analyze data in Excel. Excel users love this tool because of two main reasons, this tool is very fast, and it always gives an accurate result (as long as the data sets are correct). Let's understand this tool in detail with examples.

What is Pivot Table?

To understand what a pivot table is, let's first understand what is *Pivot*? A pivot is the central point about which something turns. Suppose you are sitting in a room with has a door and. If the door is closed in front of you, then it would look like a flat surface to you, but the moment you open it and turn it towards yourself, it will look like a straight line. But in the end, it will remain a door whether it's open or closed. This analysis of a door leads to a conclusion that whenever we pivot (either open or close) a door, it will remain the same object, that is, a door. We will just get a different angle of viewing the door. This is similar to the Pivot Table option available in Excel. When we *Pivot* a dataset, that is, keep it as a center point and turn around the dataset, we will get a different angel of it. Let's try to understand the same practically in this section.

Exercise file

A workbook containing the exercise files used in this chapter for Pivot Table in Excel, is available on https://rebrand.ly/ffdbc, the file is named 5.1 Pivot Table.xlsx. You can download it and practice along.

How to create a pivot table

To create a pivot table, one can follow the steps:

1. Select the complete data.

2. Insert Tab | Tables group | PivotTable. See the following *Figure 5.1*:

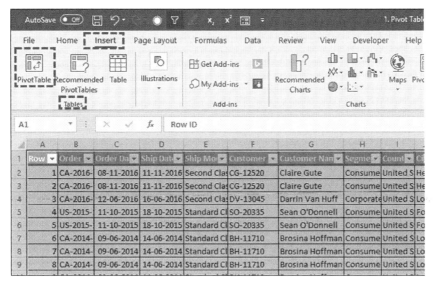

Figure 5.1

Note: Before we proceed to create a pivot table, it's important to keep the following points in mind:

1. Your data set must have meaningful headers.

2. Data set should not contain any blank row, column or even a cell.

Creating a pivot table for a real scenario

To understand how and where we can use a pivot table practically, let's consider a sample data set of around 10000 sales transactions of different product categories being sold in different regions, states and cities of the United States of America for the past 4 years.

Suppose you want to calculate the total sales amount for each category. So let's create a pivot table. Follow the standard steps to create a pivot table.

1. Select the complete data set including headers. See the following *Figure 5.2*:

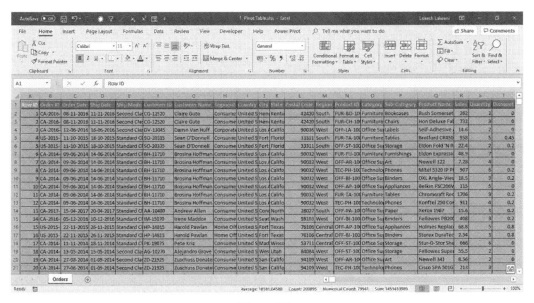

Figure 5.2

2. Under the Insert Tab select Pivot Table. This will open a dialog box. See the following *Figure 5.3*:

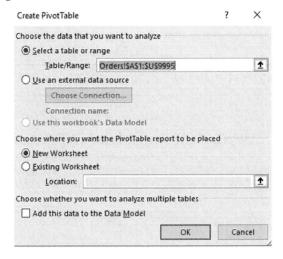

Figure 5.3

Here, you can create a pivot table in the existing worksheet by assigning a preferred location or you can create it in a new worksheet. Let's create it in a new worksheet.

3. Click Ok.

Now you have a skeleton of a pivot table. Its completely blank. On the right-hand side of the screen, you have the Field List where you can select the preferred fields to form a pivot. See the following *Figure 5.4*:

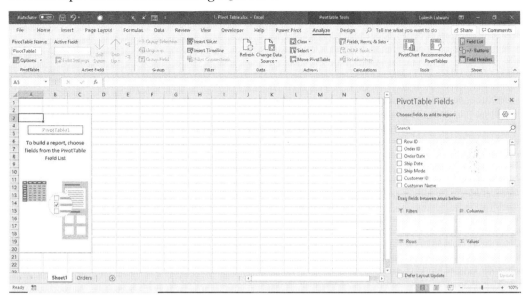

Figure 5.4

Under the Field List there are four blank boxes: Filters, Columns, Rows and Values. To form a table, we almost always need columns, rows and values. So let's start dropping the preferred fields into the respective boxes and Excel will keep forming the table on the left.

To calculate Category wise total sales, we will need two fields, that is, Category and Sales. We can drag the category from the fields into Columns or Rows.

Note: This will only change the layout; outcome will remain the same. So, you can place the fields any way you want. Here, we will drop the Category field in Rows, whereas the Sales field will go into the Values box because we need to perform calculation on it. See the following *Figure 5.5*:

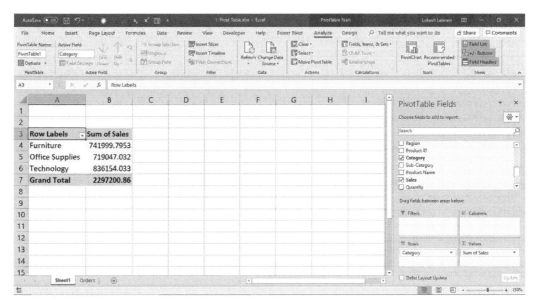

Figure 5.5

And voila! We are done! Creating a pivot table is much easier than entering complex formulas and functions. And this is just the beginning; we have lot more to cover.

Note: Field List (on the right side of the screen) is only visible when our active cell is part of the pivot table.

Calculation and grouping options

Calculation options

You must have noticed in the previous example that the moment you drop the Sales field into the Values box, Excel displays Sum of Sales automatically. What if you need to show other calculations like COUNT, AVERAGE, MAX, MIN, and so on? The answer to this is very simple. Let's say we convert Sum of Sales to Count of Sales, then we will get the total number of orders in each category. Here, we will not create another pivot table, rather we will just change the calculation of our previous pivot table from SUM to COUNT. To do so, just right-click on the any one of the figures in the table, select Summarize Values By, and then select Count. See the following *Figure 5.6*:

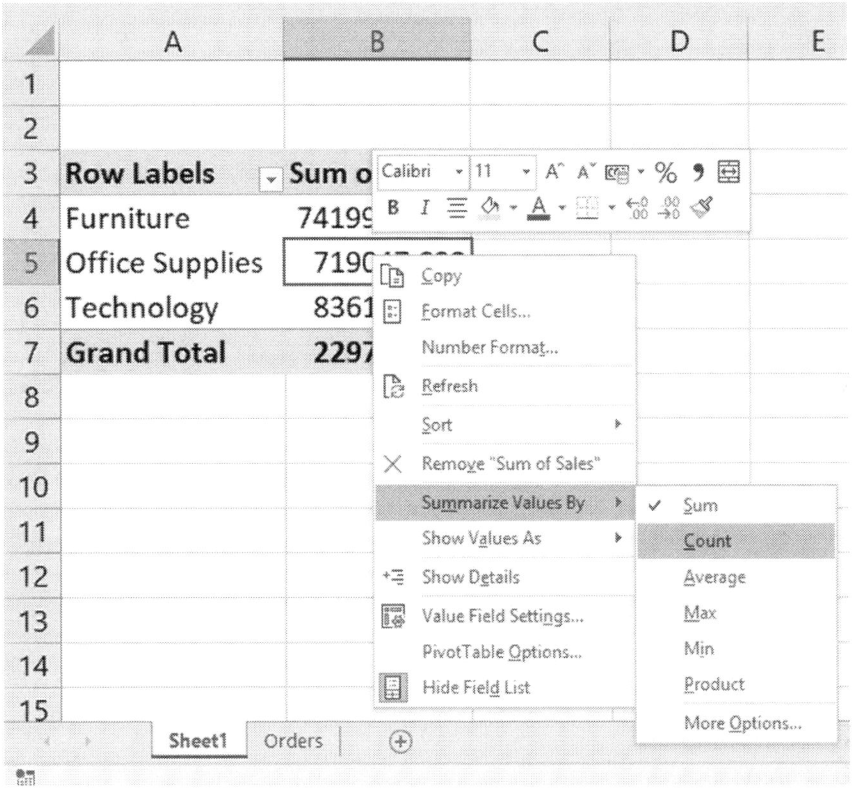

Figure 5.6

Similarly, we can use other calculation options (further calculation options are available in More Options).

Grouping options

Excel provides an amazing option in pivot tables, that is, Group. It helps in grouping data types like date, time and numbers. For example, suppose you want to group *Segment wise yearly and quarterly sales according to ship date*. Let's create a new pivot table by following the same steps mentioned previously. Now you have a blank table. As discussed earlier, let's use the fields required to solve this scenario, that is, Segment, Ship Date and Sales. Let's drop the Ship Date field in Rows, Segment in Columns and Sales in the Values box. See the following *Figure 5.7*:

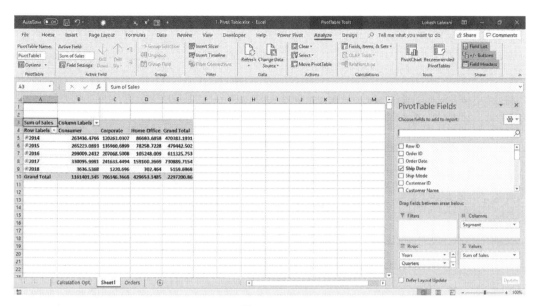

Figure 5.7

By default, Excel will show a table with years (as shown above). To change this default grouping, just right-click on any one of the years and choose **Group**. This will pop-up a box. Select the desired options, that is, Years and Quarters. And then click **Ok**. See the following *Figure 5.8*:

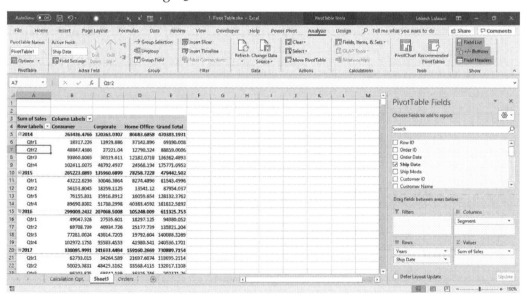

Figure 5.8

You will see how smoothly Excel has grouped the dates, which could take hours otherwise.

Report filter pages

Did you ever come across a situation where you want to break down your data into multiple sheets on the basis of a certain field? Pivot Table gives you an option to do so with just a in few clicks. Let's consider a scenario where you would like to *Prepare State wise customer sales report on individual sheets*. Let's create a pivot table for the same using Customer, State, Sales and Category (optional) fields. See the following *Figure 5.9*:

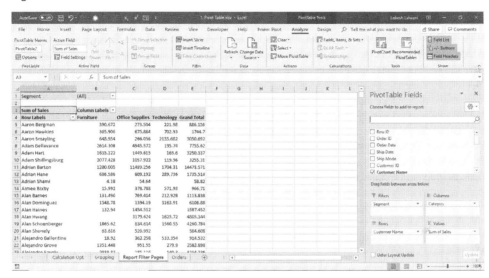

Figure 5.9

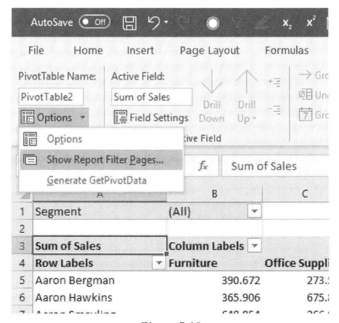

Figure 5.10

A dialog box will pop up, with all the fields in the filter box like Segment in this case. See the following *Figure 5.11*:

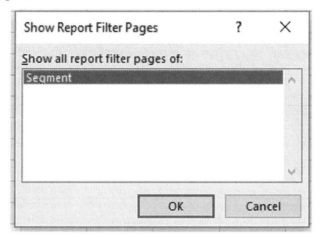

Figure 5.11

Click Ok. This will create all the following sheets as shown in *Figure 5.12*:

١t	1423.4856	133.536	938.37	2495.3916
Allen	475.3	625.272	689.94	1790.512
Roberts		119.706	145.158	264.864
iter	355.63	5612.85	639.968	6608.448
١e Ratner	51.75	36.4		88.15
١ood	202.16	51.204	292.96	728.504

Calculation Opt. | Grouping | **Consumer** | Corporate | Home Office | Report Filter P₁ ...

Type here to search

Figure 5.12

Calculated field

This helps in creating additional fields based on existing calculated fields. This makes our pivot table more powerful. Let's take an example where a 10% discount is to be given on sales of value more than 2000. So, let's create a new pivot table with the fields Order ID and Sales. See the following *Figure 5.13*:

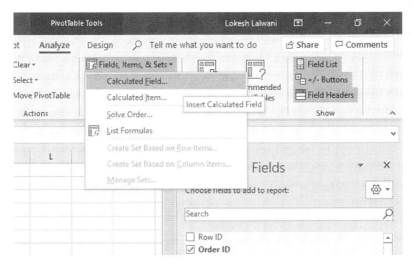

Figure 5.13

To create a calculated field, go to Analyze tab, select the Calculation group, then Fields, Items & Sets, and finally select Calculated Field…. See the following *Figure 5.14*:

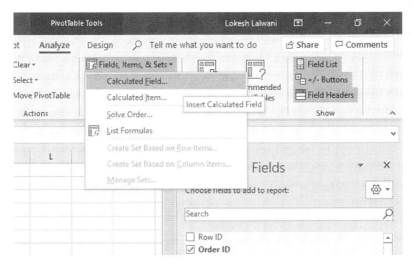

Figure 5.14

This will trigger the Insert Calculated Field dialog box. Here you need to assign a name to the new field and write a function as shown in the following *Figure 5.15*:

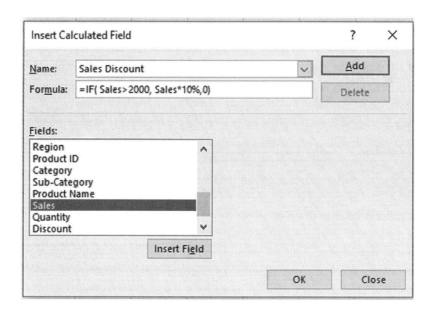

Figure 5.15

This will add a new field in our pivot table. See the following *Figure 5.16*:

Row Labels	Sum of Sales	Sum of Sales Discount
CA-2014-145317	23661	2366
CA-2016-118689	18337	1834
CA-2017-140151	14052	1405
CA-2017-127180	13716	1372
CA-2014-139892	10540	1054
CA-2017-166709	10500	1050
CA-2014-116904	9900	990
CA-2016-117121	9893	989
US-2016-107440	9135	914
CA-2016-158841	8805	881
CA-2016-143714	8539	854
CA-2014-143917	8319	832

Figure 5.16

Power Pivot and Power Query

Power Pivot is an Excel add-in that can be used to perform some cutting-edge information investigation and create complex information models. It can deal with substantial volumes of information (millions of data records) from different sources and the majority of this inside a single Excel document. Power Pivot is essentially an SSAS engine made accessible by an in-memory process that runs straightforwardly in Excel. It is commonly known as an **Internal Data Model**. The best way to collaborate with the Internal Data Model is to utilize the Power Pivot ribbon interface.

Once the Power Pivot add-in is installed and accessible, you can create a data model, which is a collection of tables with connections. Any information you import into Excel or have in Excel is accessible in the Power Pivot window through the data model. The Power Pivot ribbon gives you extra capacities well beyond the standard Excel Data tab.

Power Query is used whenever you import or connect to any data source. This helps in cleaning and transforming the data. It can be accessed through Power Pivot.

How and where to use Power Pivot and Power Query

Now that we know what Power Pivot and Power Query are all about, let's understand how exactly we can use these powerful add-ins.

Power Pivot acts as a data model. This implies that the initial step is to import data (if it is not in your Excel sheet). We will require a connector to associate with various types of data sources and import your information. This can be complex, depending on the data source.

After connecting to the data source, Excel will open another window, that is, Power Query (Query editor). Here we can just clean up the connected data and transform the same.

Once we are done with the preceding step, we will load it. Now onwards, the cleaned up data is accessible from the Pivot Table window. Here we will start building relationship between multiple data tables. We can also create multiple calculated fields and access **KPI's** (**Key Performance Indicators**).

Final step is to create a dashboard using those measures and calculated fields built using Power Pivot.

Let's now look at how to launch Power Pivot (Note: Power Query add-in need not be installed in Excel 2019 or Office 365, as this automatically opens up when we use the Get Data feature):

1. Go to the File tab, open Options, and select Add-Ins.

2. In the drop-down list under Manage: select COM Add-ins and then Go....
   See the following *Figure 5.17*:

Figure 5.17

3. Check the Microsoft Power Pivot for Excel box, and then click Ok. If you
   have other versions of the Power Pivot add-in installed, those versions are
   also listed in the COM Add-ins list.

4. Once Power Pivot is enabled, you'll have a tab named PowerPivot and you'll
   be able to see the options when you click on it. See the following *Figure 5.18*:

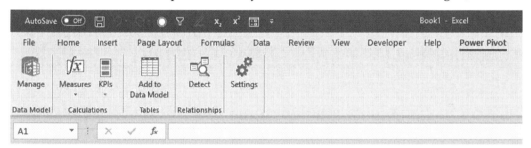

Figure 5.18

Uploading million plus data records into Power Query

Data can be uploaded to Power Query either by using an existing table in Excel or by
importing the same from a different source. As we are talking about millions of data
rows, which is beyond Excel's capacity, we will be connecting it with "MS Access"
database file. To do the same let's follow the procedure:

Exercise file

A workbook containing the exercise files used in this chapter for Power Pivot &
Power Query in Excel, is available on https://rebrand.ly/ffdbc, the file is named 5.2
Power Pivot Sample Data.accdb. You can download it and practice along.

1. Under the Data tab, go to Get Data, select From Database, and then select
   From Microsoft Access Database. See the following *Figure 5.19*:

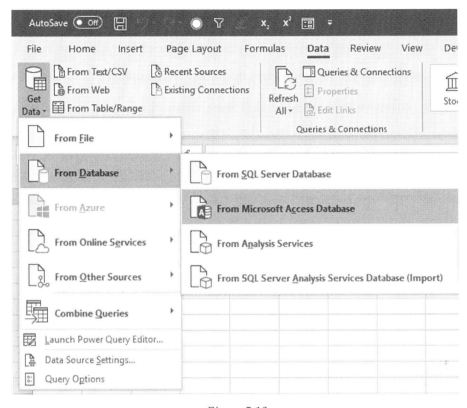

Figure 5.19

2. Browse the MS Access database file and click Import. (This will start building a connection and trigger a Navigator window).

3. Select the files to be added to the data model. Click Edit. This will pop up the Query Editor window. See the following *Figure 5.20*:

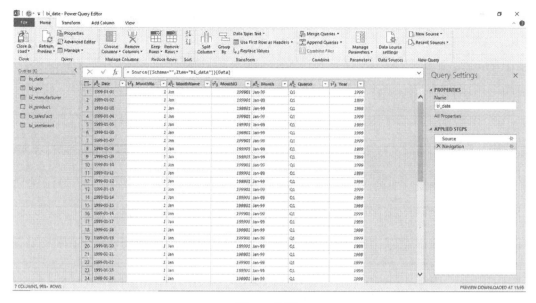

Figure 5.20

4. To check the number of rows of data in a table, we can perform a very simple task, that is, count. Go to bi_salesFact table and select the Revenue column. Then under the Transform tab, go to the Number Column group, then Statistics, and then select Count. The outcome is over a million rows. See the following *Figure 5.21*:

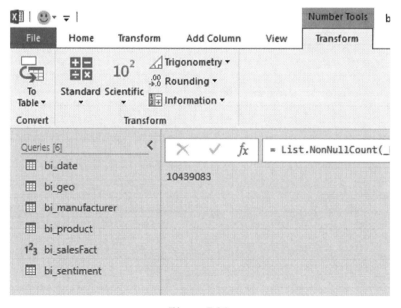

Figure 5.21

To bring the data back, just cross the latest applied step on the right side of the screen.

This is just a glimpse of how Power Query works. You can do a lot more in this window, such as unpivot columns, remove or add column, filling down or up, and removing blank rows from data, and so on.

Loading connection through Power Query

After cleaning and transforming data, let's load the connection so that now it can be accessed in Power Pivot. To do so follow these steps:

1. Under the Home tab (Query Editor), select the Close & Load dropdown, and then Close & Load To... (see the following *Figure 5.22*):

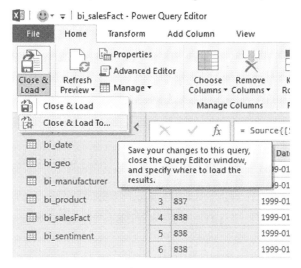

Figure 5.22

This will trigger Import Data dialog box.

2. Select Only Create Connection and check Add this data to the Data Model. See the following *Figure 5.23*:

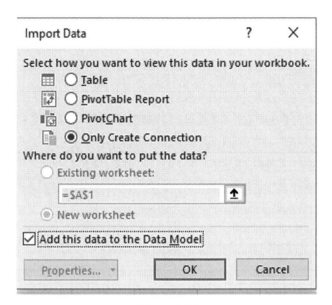

Figure 5.23

This will open a Queries & Connection pane on the right side of the screen and will show all the table names as queried. You can close this pane. Now onwards, these data table will be accessible to Power Pivot.

Accessing data in Power Pivot

Let's take a look at the data in Power Pivot view. Go to the Power Pivot tab (Note: If this tab is not visible in your Excel ribbon then you need to activate this add-in by following the steps mentioned at the start of this section), and select Manage. You will now see the data in the Power Pivot window. See the following *Figure 5.24*:

Exercise file

A workbook containing the exercise files used in this chapter for Power Pivot & Power Query in Excel, is available on https://rebrand.ly/ffdbc, the file is named 5.2 Power Pivot & Power Query.xlsx. You can download it and practice along.

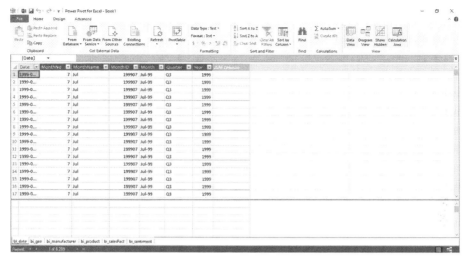

Figure 5.24

Building relationships

This is the most crucial step in creating data models in Power Pivot. Only after creating relationships, you can easily analyze data from multiple data tables. You can create a relationship in different ways but the easiest is through Diagram view under the Home tab. Once you enter this view, you will see all the data tables. You can to arrange all the lookup tables (that is, date table, geo, manufacturer and product) previously and the data tables (that is, following Sales & Sentiment table). See the following *Figure 5.25*:

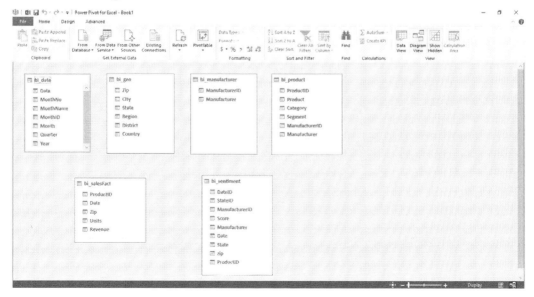

Figure 5.25

To build relationships among these tables, you can just start picking fields from lookup tables (arranged previously) and dropping onto the respective field in the data tables (arranged as follows). For example, you can build the following relationships:

- Date field from bi_date table to date field in bi_salesfact table.

- Product ID field from bi_product table to Product ID field in bi_salesfact table.

- Date field from bi_date" table to date field in bi_sentiment table.

- Manufacturer ID field from bi_ Manufacturer table to Manufacturer ID field in bi_sentiment table.

All the preceding relationships will have *One to Many* cardinality i.e. these appear only once in the lookup tables (arranged previously) and many times in the data tables (arranged as follows). See the following *Figure 5.26*:

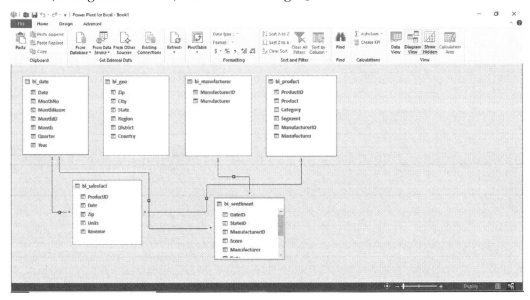

Figure 5.26

Creating calculated columns in Power Pivot

Columns can be formed/derived on the basis of calculations used in other fields from the same or other related tables. For example, in the "bi_salesfact" table, if revenue is above 300 then a discount of 10% should be given. To create this column, follow the below steps.

1. Activate the bi_salesfact table sheet tab.

2. Double click on the Add Column header and rename the same to Discount.

3. In the Function bar above, type the following function.

```
=IF(bi_salesFact[Revenue]>300,bi_salesFact[Revenue]*0.10,0)
```

4. Press *Enter* to get the outcome.

5. See the following *Figure 5.27*:

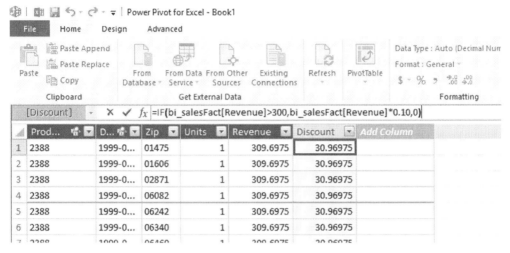

Figure 5.27

Importing data from Power Pivot in to Excel sheet

Finally, after building relationships and creating calculated columns, you can extract out the data in the form of either Pivot Tables or Pivot Charts. This eventually helps in creating a dashboard from huge amount of data, and you can pick up fields from any related table. To do so, go to the Home tab in the Power Pivot window and click on Pivot Table. This will trigger a dialog box Create Pivot Table. Here, you can create a pivot in a new worksheet or in an existing worksheet. Choose the preferred option and click Ok. Now the pivot Table fields on the right side of the window will have all the tables and fields. You can access any field from any related table to form a pivot table or chart. In the previous example, we know that the bi_salesfact table is related to the bi_product table. So let's try to identify the product category wise revenue. Here we will take the Category field from the bi_product table and drop into rows and the Revenue field from the bi_salesfact table and drop into Values. Under the Analyze tab, click on the Pivot Chart option to form a chart based on the pivot table. See the following *Figure 5.28*:

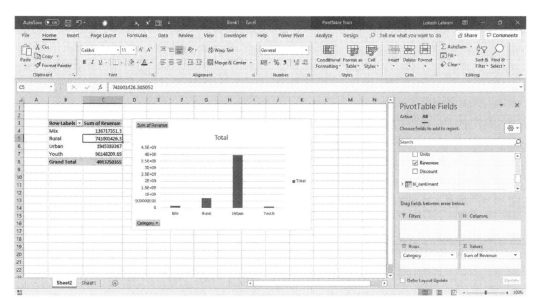

Figure 5.28

In this manner, you can use Power Pivot and Power Query to play around with huge amounts of data and create complex data models and analyze them using pivot table or pivot chart.

What-If Analysis

This tool allows you to try out different scenarios for formulas. You can choose the one that suits your need and use it for further analysis.

Three What-If Analysis options are available in Excel: Scenario Manager, Goal Seek, and Data Table. Scenario Manager and Data Table are used to decide possible outcomes from sets of information. A Data Table works with just a single or two variables, yet it can acknowledge a wide range of values for those factors. A Scenario Manager can have various variable; however it can only entertain up to 32 values. On the other hand, Goal Seek is a reverse approach, where we know the output of a scenario and would like to know any one of the inputs.

For more advanced models, we will be discussing the Analysis ToolPak later in this chapter.

Exercise file

A workbook containing the exercise files used in this chapter for What-If Analysis & Solver in Excel, is available on https://rebrand.ly/ffdbc, the file is named 5.3 What if Analysis & Solver.xlsx. You can download it and practice along.

Goal Seek (a reverse approach)

As already mentioned, this is a reverse approach, that is, we already have an output with us and we want one of the inputs to get that output. For example, if you want to apply for a loan, you will plan your expenses in such a way that you come up with a fixed amount to pay as **EMI** (**Equated monthly installments**). Because an EMI is the output of any loan calculation, the points you will be concerned about are the rate of interest, tenure, eligible loan amount, and so on, which are several inputs to arrive at an output, that is, an EMI.

Goal seek is very useful in financial modelling, sales/revenue/profit prediction, business KPI prediction, and so on.

Let's consider a simple and practical example to understand this powerful feature. Suppose, you are working as a sales representative in a company, and the company has already decided your commission rate, that is, at 2.5% of your total sales. As a highly enthusiastic sales representative, you may have decided to take $200 as commission this month. So now you want to know the amount of sales you need to do in the month to achieve your targeted commission. In this case, Sales Amount is an input and Commission Value amount is the output. So you have your output in your mind but one of the inputs, that is, Sales Amount is missing. Goal Seek can help you find the same within seconds. See the following *Figure 5.29*:

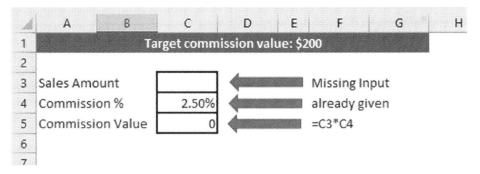

Figure 5.29

Note: For calculating the commission value, we have already written a function, which is multiplying sales amount with commission percentage. It's important to follow a rule while using Goal Seek, that the input cell should be independent and the output cell should be dependent or calculated.

To apply the Goal Seek in the preceding scenario and get the sales amount, follow the steps:

1. Under the Data tab, go to Forecast group, then What-If Analysis, and then Goal Seek. This will trigger Goal Seek dialogue box.

2. Step 2: Fill up the following:

   - Set cell: $C$5

   - To value: 200

   - By changing cell: $C$3

See the following *Figure 5.30*:

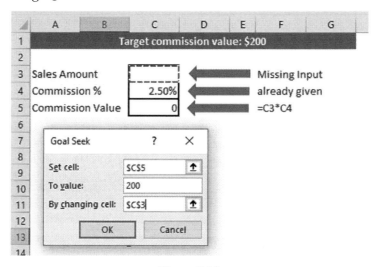

Figure 5.30

3. Click Ok. See the following *Figure 5.31*:

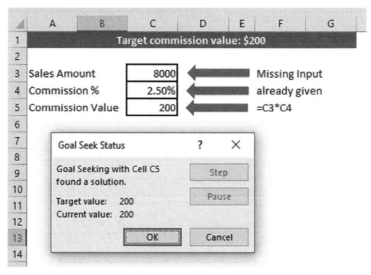

Figure 5.31

Thus, as per Goal Seek, you need to achieve $8000 of sales amount to score $200 commission. By clicking Ok we will accept the changes done by Goal Seek in cell C3 and Cancel will discard any changes.

Data Table

If you have multiple scenarios to check on the data then Data Table is the right choice for you. You can create two types of data tables, that is, one way data table (which supports only one variable) and two way data table (which supports two variables).

One-variable data table

Only one variable can be supported using the one-way data table. Let's suppose you are taking a loan of $100,000 at the rate of 12% per annum for 3 years, that is, 36 months. You want to check the EMI for multiple period scenarios, for example, 12, 24, 36, and so on months. See the following *Figure 5.32*:

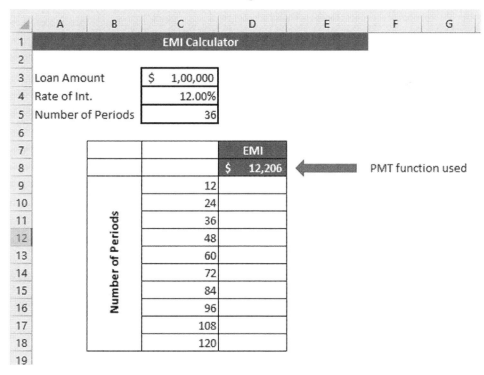

Figure 5.32

Note: The tables in the preceding figure with different scenarios of number of periods needs be created before using data table.

To use a Data Table with one variable follow the steps:

1. Select the table range C8:D18.

2. Under the Data tab, go to Forecast group, then What-If Analysis, and select Data Table.

(This will trigger the Data Table dialogue box.)

3. Row input cell will be kept blank, and Column input cell is the base number of periods, that is, cell C5 because number of periods is a variable in the following model. See the following *Figure 5.33*:

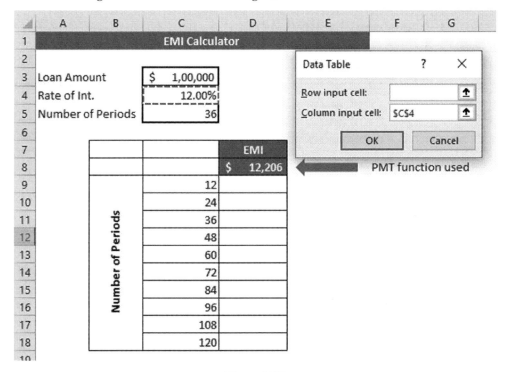

Figure 5.33

4. Click Ok.

This will fill up the complete table as shown in the following *Figure 5.34*:

◢	A	B	C	D	E	F	G
1			EMI Calculator				
2							
3	Loan Amount		$ 1,00,000				
4	Rate of Int.		12.00%				
5	Number of Periods		36				
6							
7				EMI			
8				$ 12,206	⟵ PMT function used		
9			12	$ 16,144			
10			24	$ 12,846			
11		*Number of Periods*	36	$ 12,206			
12			48	$ 12,052			
13			60	$ 12,013			
14			72	$ 12,003			
15			84	$ 12,001			
16			96	$ 12,000			
17			108	$ 12,000			
18			120	$ 12,000			
19							

Figure 5.34

Two-variable data table

This type of data table supports two variables. Let's extend the above example to calculate EMI's based on two variables, that is, Number of Periods and Rate of Int.. See the following *Figure 5.35*:

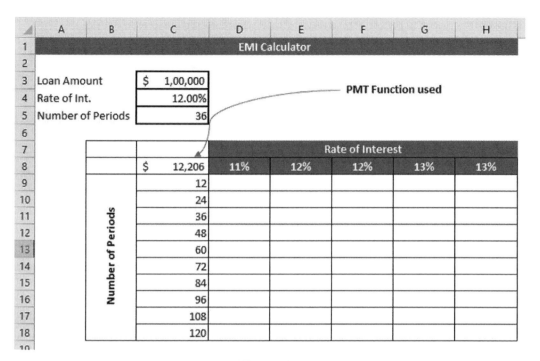

Figure 5.35

To apply a two variable data table, follow the steps:

1. Select range C8:H18.

2. Under the Data tab, go to Forecast group, then What-If Analysis, and then select Data Table.

(This will trigger the Data Table dialogue box.)

3. Row input cell is the base rate of interest, that is, cell C4 and Column input cell is the base number of periods, that is, cell C5. See the following *Figure 5.36*:

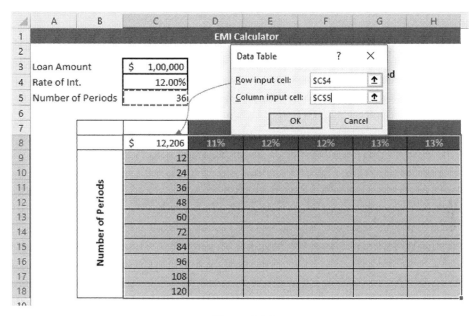

Figure 5.36

4. Click Ok.

This will fill up the complete table as shown in the following *Figure 5.37*:

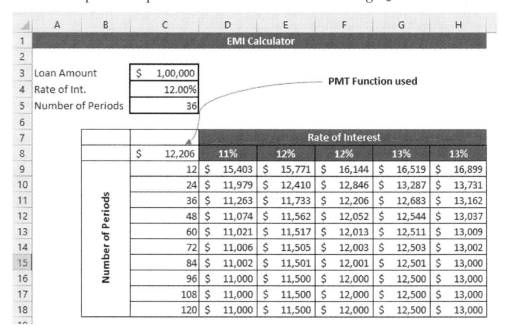

Figure 5.37

Scenario Manager

Scenario Manager helps in storing multiple values for the same set of cells; in other words, you can create different cases or scenarios by specifying different sets of values for each case referring to the same cells. We can switch between cases or scenarios to change the values in those cells. The best part of using this Excel feature is that we can compare all the scenarios at the same time.

Let's take the same example as that in the Goal Seek. Here the sales representative would be interested in knowing at a commission rate of *y* percent, how much commission he will earn if he does sale of *x* amount. So, let's create two scenarios: *High commission* (where sales value will be $10,000 and commission rate will be 3%) and *Low Commission* (where sales value will be $8,000 and commission rate will be 2%). Later we will also be comparing these values. To get to these values, let's use two variables: Sales Amount and Commission %.

Follow the following steps:

1. Under the Data tab, go to the Forecast group, then What-If Analysis, and select Scenario Manager. This will trigger a dialog box as shown in the following *Figure 5.38*:

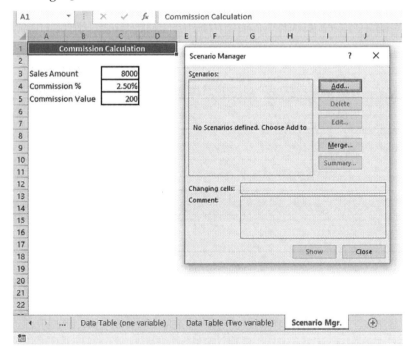

Figure 5.38

2. Click Add....

3. Assign the Scenario name as High Commission and set Changing cells as
    $C$3:$C$4. Click Ok and then change the sales value from existing $8000 to
    $10,000 and Commission % from 0.025 to 0.03. Click Add. See the following
    Figure 5.39:

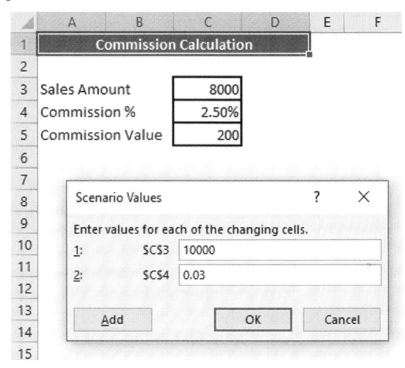

Figure 5.39

4. Add the other scenario by assigning the Scenario name as Low Commission
    and set Changing cells same as $C$3:$C$4. Click Ok. Keeping the sales
    value same as $8000 change the Commission rate from 0.025 to 0.02. Click
    Ok. (See figure 5.40 below).

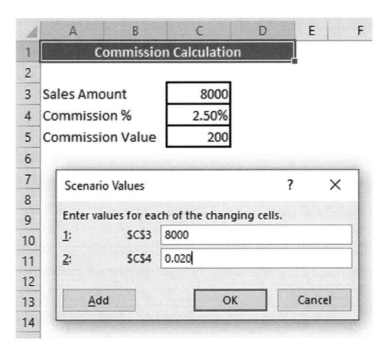

Now you will see the complete list of all the scenarios you created and you can choose to show any of them at one time. As mentioned previously, you can also compare all the scenarios. For this, click on the Summary... button on the right (see the following *Figure 5.41*):

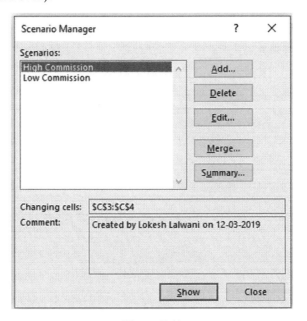

Figure 5.41

Keeping the Scenario Summary option selected, for Result Cells select cell C5 , that is, commission value in this example. Click Ok. This will create another worksheet having both the scenarios mentioned in the table with respective outcomes. (See the following *Figure 5.42*):

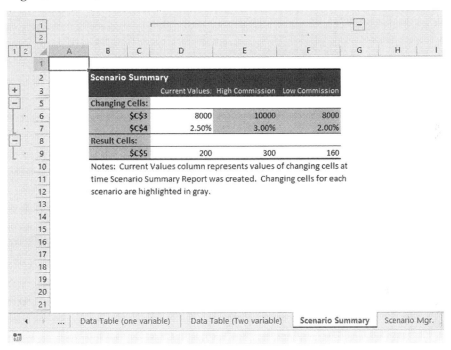

Figure 5.42

As you can see in the preceding figure that as per Result Cells, the High Commission scenario value will be $300 and the Low Commission scenario value is $160. This way we can create multiple scenarios.

Solver

Solver is an add-in that is available in Excel but may not be activated. This add-in is useful to perform What-If Analysis. It works more or less the same as Goal Seek and Scenario Manager but here you can also specify constraints or conditions. For example, a bike manufacturer is manufacturing three types of bikes and wants to know how many units of each type of bike he should produce to get the maximum profit, because he has limited resources to devote. He also has various other conditions to consider. For example, the demand for a particular bike type may be high but its profit margin is low; on the other hand another bike type has a very small market size but its profit margin is high. For all this, he can rely on the Solver add-in.

Let's first activate the add-in. Follow the steps:

1. Under the File tab, go to Options and select Add-ins.

2. Under Manage, select Excel-Add-ins and then click on Go.... See the following *Figure 5.43*:

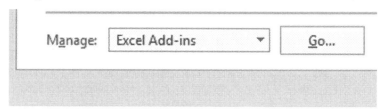

Figure 5.43

3. Check Solver Add-In and click Ok.

Now under the Data tab, you can see the add-in on the top right corner. (See the following *Figure 5.44*):

Figure 5.44

Now let's see how we can use this powerful add-in to solve a business problem:

In our example, the plant capacity of this bike manufacturer is around 1000 units in total for all the bikes in a given period. As per the last period, the manufacturer has produced the bikes in following numbers to get the desired profit (refer the following *Table 5.1*):

Product	# of Units	Profit Per Unit	Total Profit
Mountain Bike	400	$ 80	$ 32,000
Road Bike	500	$ 30	$ 15,000
Cyclocross Bike	100	$ 120	$ 12,000
Total	1000		$ 59,000

Table 5.1

Now the manufacturer wants to know what would be the perfect combination of number of units to produce to get the maximum profit. As per the preceding table, it's a very straight-forward: put all the resources in "**Cyclocross Bike**", which has highest profit margin. However, this is not feasible, because there may not be much demand for this product in the market. So, to make our example more realistic, let's use the following constraints (refer the following *Table 5.2*):

Product	Constraints
Mountain Bike	>=200
Road Bike	>=300
Cyclocross Bike	<=250

Table 5.2

As per the preceding table, he should produce 200 plus units of **Mountain Bike**, 300 plus units of **Road Bike** and not more than 250 units of **Cyclocross Bike** as per the demand in the market. So, let's see how to solve this using the Solver add-in.

1. Under the Data tab, select Solver (this will trigger a Solver dialog box).

2. Fill in the following data:

   - Set Objective: SDS7

   - To: Select Max (because it's profit. You can go with Min in case of cost or defect etc.)

   - By Changing Variable Cells: $B$4:$B$6

3. Click Add.

Here we will add our first constraint as:

Constraint 1: See the following *Figure 5.45*:

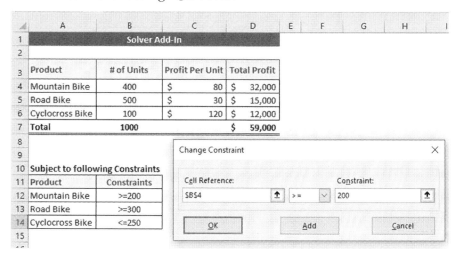

Figure 5.45

Click Add.

Constraint 2: See the following *Figure 5.46*:

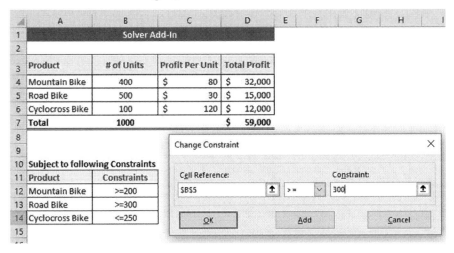

Figure 5.46

Click "Add".

Constraint 3: See the following *Figure 5.47*:

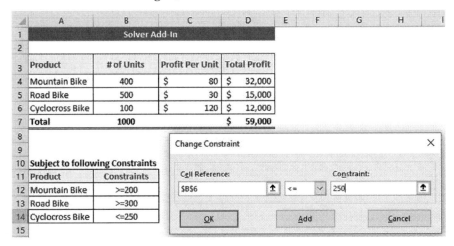

Figure 5.47

Click Add.

Constraint 4: See the following *Figure 5.48*.

(Note: This constraint was not listed in the preceding Constraints table, but it needs to be defined, the total number of units should be 1000, which is the capacity of the manufacturing plant, otherwise Excel may assume it to be any number to increase the profit).

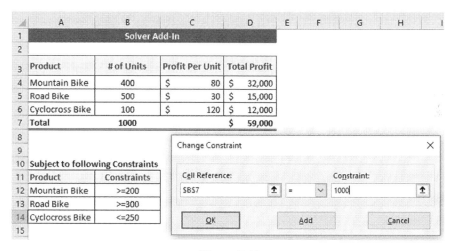

Figure 5.48

Click Ok.

Now Excel will show the total profit is $59,000. When we will click on Solve this figure will change as per our model.

4. Click Solve.

Now the profit increases to $75,000. (See the following *Figure 5.49*):

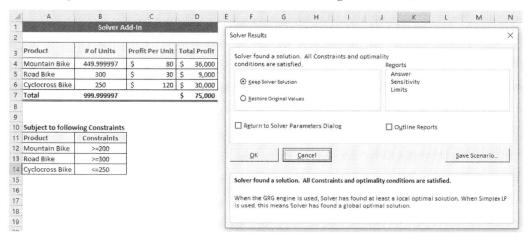

Figure 5.49

As you can see, the number of units for "**Mountain Bike**" is not a whole number. You can change it manually. Clicking Ok will accept the change and clicking Cancel will revert the change. Similarly, you can also generate reports such as Answer, Sensitivity and Limits for further details.

Analysis ToolPak

Analysis ToolPak has built-in statistical or engineering macro functions. You just need to provide the data and parameters for each analysis and this add-in will quickly and conveniently provide the appropriate outputs.

Exercise file

A workbook containing the exercise files used in this chapter for Analysis Toolpak in Excel, is available on https://rebrand.ly/ffdbc, the file is named 5.4 Analysis Tool Pak.xlsx. You can download it and practice along.

Activate Analysis ToolPak add-in

The steps to activate this add-in are the same as those for the Solver add-in.

1. Under the File tab, select Options and then Add-ins.

2. Under Manage, select Excel Add-ins and then click on Go....

3. Check Analysis ToolPak and click Ok.

Now, you should be able to see the Data Analysis option under the Data tab on the right. See the following *Figure 5.50*:

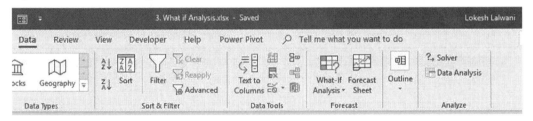

Figure 5.50

Components of Analysis ToolPak

The following list of statistical, financial and engineering tools are available in this pack:

*   Anova
*   Correlation
*   Covariance

- Descriptive Statistics
- Exponential Smoothing
- F-Test Two-Sample for Variances
- Fourier Analysis
- Histogram
- Moving Average
- Random Number Generation
- Rank and Percentile
- Regression
- Sampling
- t-Test
- z-Test

Analyzing data using ToolPak

As you can see this tool pack offers several tools to analyze almost any data set. Let's try this great add-in by using one of the tools: Descriptive Statistics. Consider a data set of students with their respective scores in their third semester exams (*Figure 5.51*).

Let's perform descriptive statistics on this list of scores to analyze the data.:

1. Under the Data tab select Data Analysis.

2. Select Descriptive Statistics and click Ok. This will open the Descriptive Analysis dialog box).

3. Fill in the following data:

   - Input Range (select all the scores): $B$3:$B$18.
   - Output Range: $D$2.
   - Summary statistics: Tick mark this box.

See the following *Figure 5.51*:

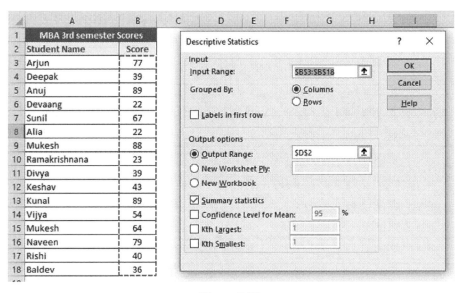

Figure 5.51

Click Ok.

And your task is done. (Refer the following *Table 5.3*):

Column1	
Mean	54.4375
Standard Error	6.166420322
Median	48.5
Mode	39
Standard Deviation	24.66568129
Sample Variance	608.3958333
Kurtosis	-1.48542443
Skewness	0.162874803
Range	67
Minimum	22
Maximum	89
Sum	871
Count	16

Table 5.3

A list of most common Descriptive Statistics is performed by the Analysis ToolPak in a few clicks. You can similarly explore the rest of the tools in this amazing add-in.

Forecast Sheet

It helps in creating a new sheet containing the forecast based on historical time-based data. It creates both tables and charts showing historical as well as predicted values. This tool is helpful in predicting sales, cost, inventory requirement, and so on.

Exercise file

A workbook containing the exercise files used in this chapter for Forecast Sheet in Excel, is available on https://rebrand.ly/ffdbc, the file is named 5.5 Forecast Sheet. xlsx. You can download it and practice along.

How to use this feature

First, you must have time-based data. In our example, we will use the monthly sales data for 2 years (see the following *Figure 5.52*) and predict sales for the next year on the basis of these previous values:

	A	B	C
1	**Monthly Sales**		
2	Date	Sales	
3	01-01-2017	$ 6,083	
4	01-02-2017	$ 5,564	
5	01-03-2017	$ 9,348	
6	01-04-2017	$ 5,561	
7	01-05-2017	$ 7,379	
8	01-06-2017	$ 7,447	
9	01-07-2017	$ 7,017	
10	01-08-2017	$ 6,851	
11	01-09-2017	$ 6,180	
12	01-10-2017	$ 7,223	
13	01-11-2017	$ 6,361	
14	01-12-2017	$ 6,991	
15	01-01-2018	$ 6,480	
16	01-02-2018	$ 6,160	
17	01-03-2018	$ 9,921	
18	01-04-2018	$ 8,132	
19	01-05-2018	$ 8,004	
20	01-06-2018	$ 8,637	
21	01-07-2018	$ 8,905	
22	01-08-2018	$ 9,652	
23	01-09-2018	$ 5,968	

Forecast Sheet ⊕

Ready

Figure 5.52

Follow the steps to use the Forecast Sheet option:

1. Select the data including headers.

2. Under the Data tab select Forecast Sheet.

Note: By default, Excel may show a forecast for next 6 months but as we need it for a complete year, we can change the Forecast End date.

Change Forecast End data to 1st Dec 2019.

You will see a straight line for forecast. See the following *Figure 5.53*:

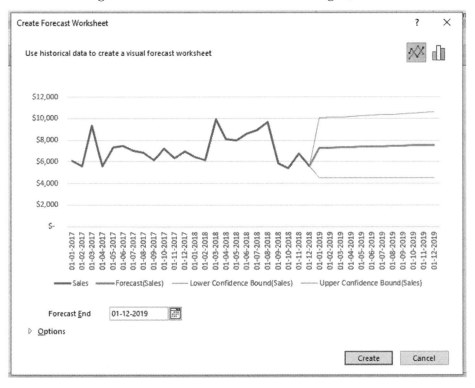

Figure 5.53

This means that the forecast line is not capturing the seasonality (ups and downs in the past). Therefore, we need to edit the seasonality option accordingly.

3. Click on Options. Set the Seasonality from 0 to 12. This will consider the past trend (ups and downs). See the following *Figure 5.54*:

Figure 5.54

You can see three orange color lines in the preceding figure. The thicker one is the forecast line, and thinner ones represent the confidence interval that is, our forecasted sales will fall in between these lines only. If we increase the confidence level percentage, the gap in between them will increase. As of now let's keep it as it is.

4. Click Create.

This will bring in a new sheet with a table having historical as well as forecasted data with a chart. See the following *Figure 5.55*:

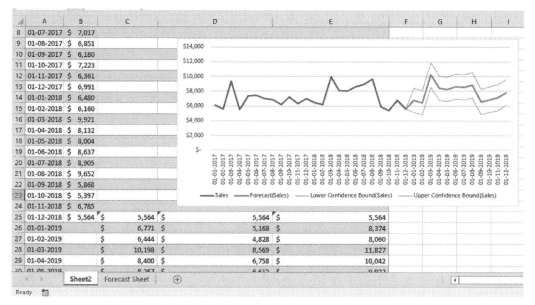

Figure 5.55

Summary

After understanding these amazing data analysis tools present in Excel you can easily and effectively analyze your data and get fruitful insights. These insights will eventually help you or your management to take important decisions related to business. Microsoft is continuously adding new features related to Data Analysis. You can further explore some of the advanced features of all the tools we have discussed in this chapter, especially Power Pivot and Analysis ToolPak.

Next chapter will talk about the amazing tools Excel offers to visualize the analyzed data. In the case of huge amounts of data, a table format isn't as impactful as an appropriate chart. Patterns, trends and correlations that might go undetected in data sets can be exposed and recognized easier with data visualization.

CHAPTER 6

Data Visualization

Graphical representation of information and data using visual elements such as charts, graphs, and maps, is known as data visualization. In case of data sets, it's almost essential to use such a visual aid be able to read the data quickly. Data visualization not only gives us a visual layout of a data set but it also helps in classifying and categorizing the data. It is difficult to recognize patterns or trends by just looking at the numbers derived from Data Analysis, but through an appropriate graph/chart, we can easily keep an eye on the trend. Even decision makers love data visualization as it saves time and presents data in a form of a story.

Let's dive into the world of data visualization and explore some of the amazing visualization elements present in Excel.

Structure:

In this chapter, we will discuss:

- Charts
- Pivot charts
- Slicers
- Sparklines
- Conditional formatting
- Power Map

Objective:

The objective of this chapter is to make you an Excel user who is not only good at analyzing data but equally good at data visualization. After going through this chapter, you will be able to create different types of charts. You will also learn how to create a pivot chart and use slicers along with it. You will get a thorough knowledge on Sparklines, and understand where and how to format data on the basis of certain conditions with Conditional Formatting. Finally, you willget a hold on a new feature of Excel: Power Map.

Charts

Excel offers a bouquet of charts such as Column, Bar, Line, Pie, Area, Surface, Waterfall, and Combo. You can choose the most appropriate chart as per the data and it takes only few clicks. Here, we will first understand how to create a chart in Excel (the steps are almost the same for all types of charts. Then we will discuss the different elements of a chart, and finally, we will explore some of the most useful charts one by one.

Exercise file

A workbook containing the exercise files used in this chapter for Charts in Excel, is available on https://rebrand.ly/ffdbc, the file is named 6.1 Charts.xlsx. You can download it and practice along.

Let's begin.

Insert a chart

There are two ways to insert a chart. You can either use shortcuts, or you can just follow the path from the ribbon to get a beautiful and informative chart.

Using shortcuts: Excel provides two shortcuts to create a chart. Using either of them will always give you a column chart, but it can further be modified to any other type of chart. Let's consider a sample data set of products and their region-wise sales. See the following *Figure 6.1*:

Product	Delhi		Mumbai		Kolkata	
			Product & Region wise Sales			
Car Seat Covers	$	1,269	$	4,762	$	1,920
LED lamps	$	4,672	$	1,638	$	4,955
Alloy Wheels	$	3,821	$	4,106	$	3,067
Total	$	9,762	$	10,506	$	9,942

Figure 6.1

To insert a chart using a shortcut, select the complete data set (ignore Total row) including field headers and press the *F11* key. See the following *Figure 6.2*:

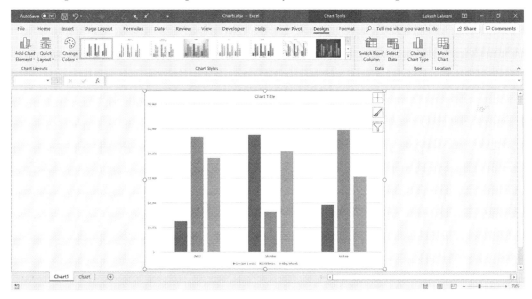

Figure 6.2

You will see a new worksheet named Chart1. This is known as a **Chart Sheet**. This chart can be moved to an existing worksheet by using the Move chart option under the Design tab.

Another shortcut to insert a chart is *Alt + F1*. This will create an embedded chart, that is, the chart will get inserted into an existing worksheet. Again, select the data as before and press *Alt + F1*. See the following *Figure 6.3*:

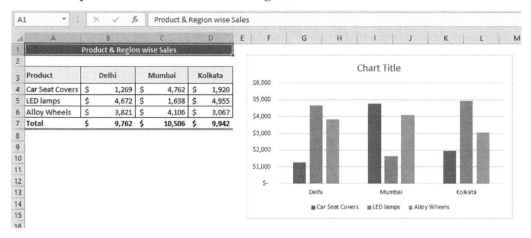

Figure 6.3

Using Insert tab: Select the data, and go to the Insert tab. Here select the Charts group, then 2-D Column, and then Clustered Column. This will give you a new chart. You can choose any appropriate chart from here.

Excel also recommends charts on the basis of the data we have selected; this is the Recommended Charts feature. Let's try it. Select the data and go to the Insert tab. Here select the Charts group and then Recommended Charts. Excel will recommend a few charts here. Most of the times, this option will satisfy your need for an appropriate chart but not always. See the following *Figure 6.4*:

Figure 6.4

Add or remove chart elements

By now you must have got a hold on inserting a chart. But you must have noticed that whenever you insert a chart, most of the elements are missing, such as the Chart Title, Axis Titles, Legend, and Data Labels. You can add them individually or choose a default where these are already loaded in a chart. It's still recommended to have a look at them individually as it is a very common requirement to either turn them On or Off. Let's carry on with the same chart we inserted earlier and add those elements one by one.

To see the most common elements of a chart, keep the chart activated and click on the + sign on the right. See the following *Figure 6.5*:

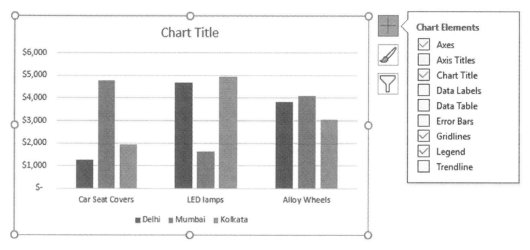

Figure 6.5

- **Axes**: This will show or hide both the axes from the chart.

- **Axis Titles**: As of now, axis titles are missing from our chart. Checking this box will turn on the default layout of axis title for both the vertical and horizontal axes. Now, you will get those titles, but you still need to change them to show the appropriate ones. You can either just click on the titles and re-write them, or you can link them with any cell too. Click on the horizontal axis title, and after pressing the "=" symbol on your keyboard, click on cell "A3" and hit the *Enter* key. The contents of the cell will start appearing in the title. For the vertical axis title, just click on the title and type Total Sales. See the following *Figure 6.6*:

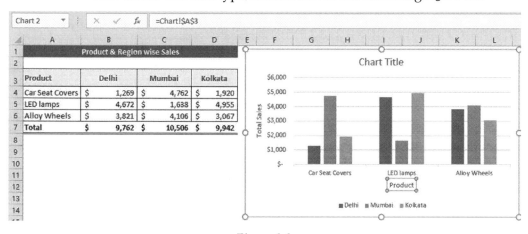

Figure 6.6

- **Chart Title:** As you can already see it in the chart, just link the same with cell A1.

- **Data Labels:** At times it's good to show the data labels on each column or bar. You can choose from several options, but as of now, let's go with *outside end* which shows data labels on the edge of each column or bar.

- **Data Table:** Enabling this option will insert the complete data table within the chart by leveraging on the horizontal axis. There are two options in this feature: with legends and without legends. It's always better to choose the with legends option as with this you can ignore the legend keys and thus save space on the chart.

- **Error Bars:** These are used to indicate any error or uncertainty in the reported measurement. They give a graphical representation of how far the actual value might be. You can customize the same by specifying both the ends. We will not be using the same in our example though.

- **Gridlines:** A chart in Excel has major and minor gridlines. You can turn them On or Off from here. As of now let's keep it as it is.

- **Legend:** It is a colored marker stating the data category in the chart. Usually it is displayed at the bottom of the chart, and it's position can be changed to top, right, or left too. As we have already activated the data table with legend key, we can simply turn the legend Off.

- **Trendline:** Excel has made it very easy to show a trendline in a chart by just checking this option. By default, it shows a linear trend, but you can choose from a list of options such as Exponential, Linear Forecast, and Moving Average. For our current data set, we will just keep it disabled.

By enabling the preceding chart elements our chart is now fully loaded. See the following *Figure 6.7*:

Figure 6.7

Furthermore, several chart styles are available under the Design tab. See the following *Figure 6.8*:

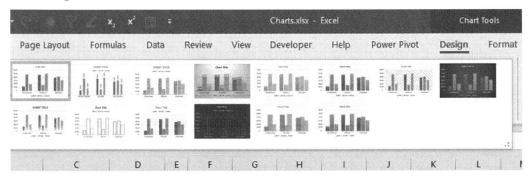

Figure 6.8

Different types of charts

Excel offers plethora of charts, where we can choose different types for different data sets. Let's understand each chart type in brief:

(Note: Of the different chart types available in Excel, Map Chart and Funnel Chart have already been discussed in the first chapter of this book)

Column and Bar charts

In Column or Bar chart, data is shown in the form of columns or bars , thus enabling comparison by column or Bar length.

Here we have a data set containing Department wise number of Employees. Column chart would be suitable for such data as we need to show a comparison between departments on the basis of number of employees in each department. See the following *Figure 6.9*:

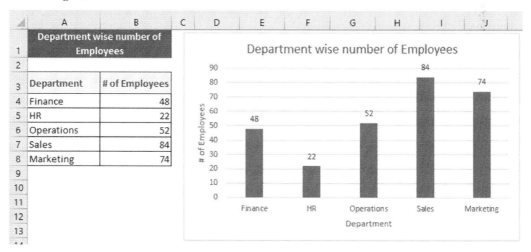

Figure 6.9

Steps to insert a chart will remain the same for all the types of charts. Let's insert a Column chart, based on the data mentioned in the preceding figure. See the following *Figure 6.10*:

Figure 6.10

Column chart category has different types of charts. Refer following *Table 6.1* for a brief understanding:

Type of Column Chart	Description
Clustered Column and 3-D Clustered Column	It shows columns in 2-D (Clustered Column) and 3-D format (3-D Clustered Column), but 3-D Clustered Column doesn't use a third value axis (depth axis)
Stacked Column and 3-D Stacked Column	It shows values in either 2-D or 3-D stacked columns, but 3-D Clustered Column doesn't use a third value axis (depth axis). This chart type is useful when there are multiple data series and the focus is on the totals.
100% Stacked Column and 3-D 100% Stacked Column	It shows values in either 2-D or 3-D stacked columns to represent 100%, but 3-D Clustered Column doesn't use a third value axis (depth axis). This chart type is suitable when there are multiple data series and the focus is on the contribution of each data series in the totals of its own category.
3-D Column	This has three axes: horizontal, vertical, and depth axes. This helps in two-way comparison, i.e., comparison between data categories and data series as well.

Table 6.1

Line chart

Line charts are primarily used to show the trend over equal intervals of time , for example, days, months, quarters, years, and so on. Let's take an example of yearly sales of an organization. A Line chart would be the best fit for this. See the following *Figure 6.11*:

◢	A	B
1	**Yearly Sales**	
2		
3	**Year**	**Sales ($ mn)**
4	2008	106
5	2009	174
6	2010	298
7	2011	269
8	2012	192
9	2013	105
10	2014	280
11	2015	251
12	2016	152
13	2017	215
14	2018	130

Figure 6.11

Here, we have inserted a simple line chart showing the trend of sales over different years. See the following *Figure 6.12*:

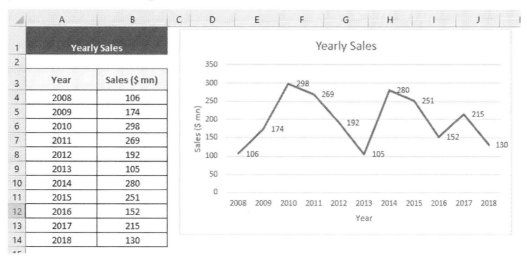

Figure 6.12

Several line chart options are available in Excel. Refer *Table 6.2* to get a brief understanding of the same.

Type of Line charts	Description
Line and Line with markers	This chart type is suitable for showing trends. Markers will be an added advantage.
Stacked Line and Stacked Line with markers	A stacked chart will show the contribution of each data point to the trend.
100% Stacked Line and 100% Stacked Line with markers	It will show the percentage contribution of each data point, which accumulates to 100% in the trend.
3-D Line	It's a 3-D line view that shows the trend.

Table 6.2

Pie and Doughnut chart

A Pie chart shows the contribution of each data point. It's suitable to insert a Pie chart in the following cases:

- You have only one data series.
- You have between 3 to 8 data points.
- None of the values are negative.

Considering the preceding points, let's take a sample data set of product-wise total sales. See the following *Figure 6.13*:

	A	B
1	Product wise Sales	
2		
3	Product	Total Sales
4	Car Seat Covers	$ 2,001
5	LED lamps	$ 2,978
6	Outer Graphics	$ 4,952
7	Upgraded Bumper	$ 1,413
8	Alloy Wheels	$ 3,260
9	**Total**	**$ 14,604**

Figure 6.13

Let's insert a Pie chart based on the given data. See the following *Figure 6.14*:

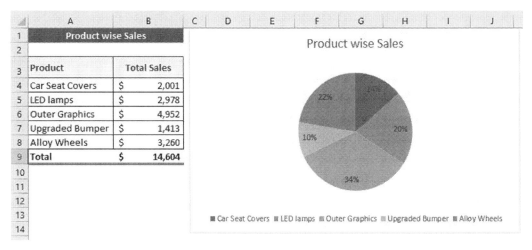

Figure 6.14

Different types of Pie charts are available in Excel. Refer *Table 6.3* below for a brief understanding:

Type of Pie Charts	Description
Pie and 3-D Pie	It shows the contribution of each value to a total in 2-D or 3-D format. We can drag the any piece of Pie out, too.
Pie of pie and Bar of Pie	In Pie or Pie we have two pies Big and small. In Bar of Pie we have a big pie and a bar. It shows the major categories in the bigger Pie and minor category of any one of the major categories in smaller Pie or Bar.

Table 6.3

Doughnut chart: Unlike Pie chart, a doughnut chart can contain more than one data series. Let's take the same example as previously and add another data series, that is, Sales for years 2017 and year 2018. See the following *Figure 6.15*:

	A	B	C
1	Product wise Sales for Year 2017 & 18		
2			
3	Product	Sales (yr. 2017)	Sales (yr. 2018)
4	Car Seat Covers	$ 2,001	$ 3,766
5	LED lamps	$ 2,978	$ 2,983
6	Outer Graphics	$ 4,952	$ 4,913
7	Upgraded Bumper	$ 1,413	$ 1,294
8	Alloy Wheels	$ 3,260	$ 1,173
9	Total	$ 14,604	$ 14,129

Figure 6.15

A Doughnut chart will look like as follows. See the following *Figure 6.16*:

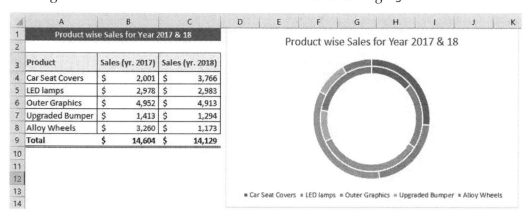

Figure 6.16

Area chart

An Area chart shows the sum of the plotted values over a period of time.

Let's take an example to show Product & Region wise Sales. See the following *Figure 6.17*:

	A	B	C	D
1		Product & Region wise Sales		
2				
3	Product	Delhi	Mumbai	Kolkata
4	Car Seat Covers	$ 1,269	$ 4,762	$ 1,920
5	LED lamps	$ 4,672	$ 1,638	$ 4,955
6	Alloy Wheels	$ 3,821	$ 4,106	$ 3,067
7	Total	$ 9,762	$ 10,506	$ 9,942

Figure 6.17

An Area chart for the same will be as follows (See the following *Figure 6.18*):

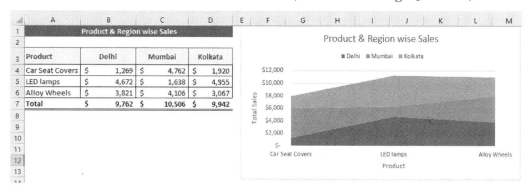

Figure 6.18

Refer the following *Table 6.4* for a brief understanding of the different types of area charts:

Type of Area charts	Description
Area and 3-D Area	It shows the trend over a period in either 2-D or 3-D.
Stacked Area and 3-D Stacked Area	It shows the trend of the contribution of each value over a period.
100% Stacked Area and 3-D 100% Stacked Area	It shows the trend of the percentage that each value contributes over a period.

X Y (Scatter) and Bubble chart

An XY chart plots two variables and shows the intersecting point in a clustered manner. This chart type is generally used to show scientific, statistical, and engineering data. Let's take an example to understand this chart type. Here we will see the impact of Discount % on the # of Units Sold. See the following *Figure 6.19*:

	A	B
1		
2	Discount %	# of Units Sold
3	2.00%	1508
4	3.00%	1803
5	0.25%	1206
6	3.85%	2005
7	4.60%	2200
8	8.30%	3500
9	4.50%	1800
10	8.50%	4500
11	5.50%	3020
12	6.00%	3450
13	7.00%	3655
14	3.00%	1698
15	2.50%	1475
16	4.00%	2405
17	9.00%	6088
18	7.00%	5438

Figure 6.19

An X Y chart on the preceding dataset will show a positive correlation between the given data series. See the following *Figure 6.20*:

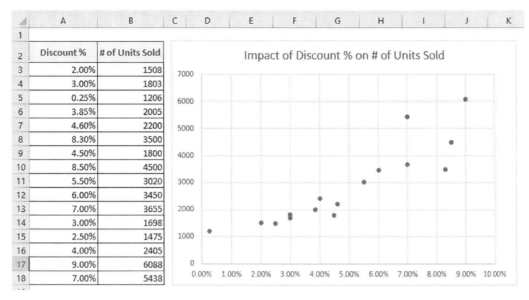

	A	B
2	Discount %	# of Units Sold
3	2.00%	1508
4	3.00%	1803
5	0.25%	1206
6	3.85%	2005
7	4.60%	2200
8	8.30%	3500
9	4.50%	1800
10	8.50%	4500
11	5.50%	3020
12	6.00%	3450
13	7.00%	3655
14	3.00%	1698
15	2.50%	1475
16	4.00%	2405
17	9.00%	6088
18	7.00%	5438

Figure 6.20

Several X Y Chart options are available in Excel. Refer the following *Table 6.5* to get a brief understanding of the same:

Type of X Y charts	Description
Scatter	It shows only the data points a dots on plotted area.
Scatter with smooth lines and markers and Scatter with smooth lines	It shows a smooth line connecting the data points. You have an option to put markers too.
Scatter with straight lines and markers and Scatter with straight lines	It shows a straight line connecting the data points. You have an option to put markers too.

Instead of data points (as in an XY Scatter chart), a bubble chart will show a bubble where, apart from the position of that bubble (which is based on the *X* and *Y*-axis values), the size of the bubble also uses a data value. Let's add sales amount to the previous XY chart example, and plot it on a Bubble chart. See the following *Figure 6.21*:

	A	B	C
1			
2	Discount %	# of Units Sold	Sales
3	2.00%	1508	8,00,289
4	3.00%	1803	9,55,601
5	0.25%	1206	4,48,526
6	3.85%	2005	9,25,981
7	4.60%	2200	5,83,260
8	8.30%	3500	7,78,017

Figure 6.21

A Bubble chart based on the preceding data will not only show the intersecting points of X and Y values but will also show the sales amount as the size of the bubble. See the following *Figure 6.22*:

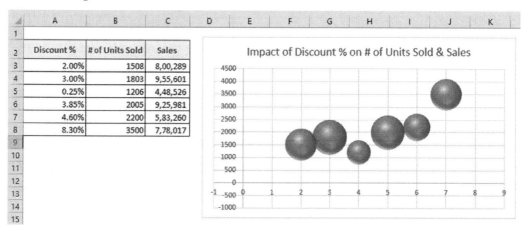

Figre 6.22

Stock chart

As the name suggests, it is used to show fluctuations in stock prices, although it can also be used to show data such as temperature and rainfall. (which comprises fluctuations). It's very important to organize the data to create a stock chart. Let's take a sample data set of stock prices of XYZ Ltd for 6 days including Open, High, Low, and Close prices on each day. See the following *Figure 6.23*:

◢	A	B	C	D	E
1			XYZ Ltd. Stock Price		
2					
3	Date	Open	High	Low	Close
4	19-03-2019	50	59	43	52
5	20-03-2019	52	58	45	54
6	21-03-2019	54	62	48	59
7	22-03-2019	59	63	42	53
8	23-03-2019	53	59	49	51
9	24-03-2019	51	64	48	53

Figure 6.23

Let's see how it looks like on a Stock chart. See the following *Figure 6.24*:

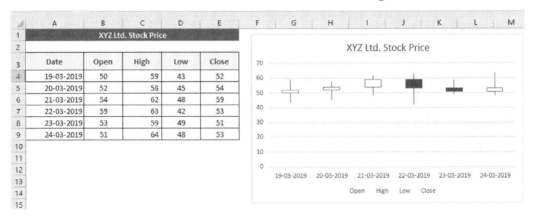

Figure 6.24

The sequence of the columns is important here. As the data set has columns in the order Open, High, Low, and Close, the columns in the chart should also be in this order. The darker ones in the preceding chart are the ones where the closing price is lesser than the opening price of that day. This type of chart is also known as a **candlestick chart** in stock markets.

Few other categories of stock charts are available in Excel. Let's have a look at the brief description of the same below. (Refer the following *Table 6.6*):

Type of Stock charts	Description
High-Low-Close	It shows High, Low, and Close data points.
Open-High-Low-Close	It shows Open, High, Low, and Close data points.
Volume-High-Low-Close	It shows High, Low, and Close values of a stock along with the volume traded in that period.

Type of Stock charts	Description
Volume-Open-High-Low-Close	It shows Open, High, Low and Close data points along with the volume of the stock traded in that period.

Surface chart

A Surface chart is used to show X, Y, Z values, colours and patterns indicate areas that are in the same range of values. Let's take some sample X, Y, Z values. See the following *Figure 6.25*:

	A	B	C	D	E	F
1			X, Y, Z Values			
2						
3	X/Y	-1	-0.5	0	0.5	1
4	-1	0.3	0.3	0.78	-1	-0.48
5	-0.5	0.2	-0.3	-0.96	0.56	-0.69
6	0	-0.5	1	0.5	0.87	-1
7	0.5	-0.3	-0.2	0.75	-0.63	0.49
8	1	-0.1	-3	0.12	-0.2	1

Figure 6.25

Inserting the above values on a Surface chart will look like the following *Figure 6.26*:

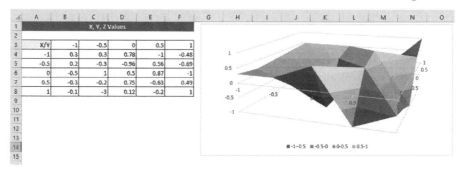

Figure 6.26

Here, the 3-D rotation option plays an important role.

Excel provides a couple of more Surface chart categories, as discussed below:

Type of Surface charts	Description
3-D Surface	It helps identify the relationships between large amounts of data that is otherwise difficult to see. Colour bands indicates the difference between the values.
Wireframe 3-D Surface	As the name suggests, it does not show colors; instead it shows a wire frame. Therefore, it's difficult to read but very easy and fast to plot huge data.
Contour	Here color bands represent specific ranges of values. The lines in a contour chart connect interpolated points of equal value.
Wireframe Contour	It's a Contour Surface chart without colours, that is, just with wires.

Radar charts

A Radar chart helps to aggregate values of several data series. It is also known as a **Spider Chart** or a **Web Chart**. It can be used to analyze performances such as target vs actuals in customer satisfaction, employee performance, and so on.

Let's take an example of target vs actual sales in different regions. See the following *Figure 6.27*:

	A	B	C
1	**Product wise Target Vs Actual Sales**		
2			
3	Product	Target Sales	Actual Sales
4	Car Seat Covers	$ 4,050	$ 3,766
5	LED lamps	$ 2,978	$ 1,898
6	Outer Graphics	$ 4,952	$ 3,913
7	Upgraded Bumper	$ 1,413	$ 1,294
8	Alloy Wheels	$ 3,260	$ 1,173
9	Total	$ 16,653	$ 12,044

Figure 6.27

The Radar chart for the preceding data will be as follows (see the following *Figure 6.28*):

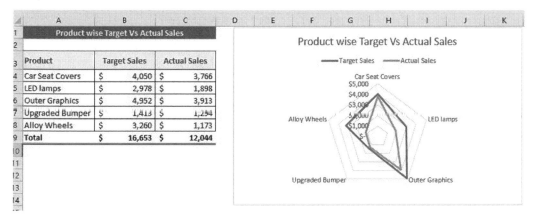

Figure 6.28

Refer the following *Table 6.8* for the different types radar charts available in Excel:

Type of Radar charts	Description
Radar and Radar with Markers	It is a Radar chart with or without markers.
Filled Radar	An area covered by a data series is filled by a color.

Treemap chart (only Office 2016 and above)

The Treemap chart provides a hierarchical view of your data and is an easy way to compare different levels of categorization. It shows data points in different sizes based on the value of the data points. It shows different categories in different colors.

Let's take an example, where we have region and product-wise sales. See the following *Figure 6.29*:

	A	B	C
1		**Region and Product wise Sales**	
2			
3	Region	Product	Sales
4	Delhi	Car Seat Covers	$ 1,269
5	Delhi	LED lamps	$ 4,762
6	Delhi	Alloy Wheels	$ 1,920
7	Mumbai	Car Seat Covers	$ 4,672
8	Mumbai	LED lamps	$ 1,638
9	Mumbai	Alloy Wheels	$ 4,955
10	Kolkata	Car Seat Covers	$ 3,821
11	Kolkata	LED lamps	$ 4,106
12	Kolkata	Alloy Wheels	$ 3,067

Figure 6.29

A Treemap chart for the preceding data will look as follows *Figure 6.30*):

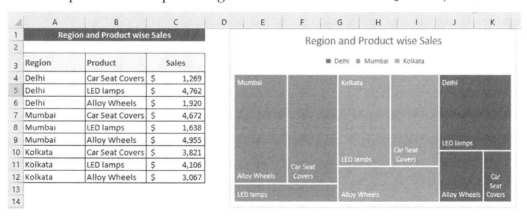

Figure 6.30

Here legends show that Mumbai and Kolkata totals are higher as compared to Delhi, because they take up more space on the chart. Also, Alloy Wheels seems to be the favorite product in Mumbai.

Note: This chart type doesn't have sub categories.

Sunburst chart (only Office 2016 and above)

A Sunburst chart is ideal for showing hierarchical data with multiple levels. It can also handle the empty cells in the data set. The inner-most circle represents the top level of the hierarchy. If only one level of hierarchy is available then a sunburst chart will look like a Doughnut chart.

Let's understand this chart type by adding one more level, that is, State, in the sample data set we used for creating a Treemap chart. (See the following *Figure 6.31*):

	A	B	C	D
1	State, Region and Product wise Sales			
2				
3	State	Region	Product	Sales
4	Delhi	Delhi	Car Seat Covers	$ 1,269
5	Delhi	Delhi	LED lamps	$ 4,762
6	Delhi	Delhi	Alloy Wheels	$ 1,920
7	Maharashtra	Mumbai		
8	Maharashtra	Mumbai	LED lamps	$ 1,638
9	Maharashtra	Mumbai	Alloy Wheels	$ 4,955
10	West Bengal	Kolkata	Car Seat Covers	$ 3,821
11	West Bengal	Kolkata	LED lamps	$ 4,106
12	West Bengal	Kolkata		

Figure 6.31

Let's remove the Car Seat covers category from Mumbai and Alloy Wheels category from Kolkata to see how this will work on a Sunburst chart. Let's insert the chart *Figure 6.32*:

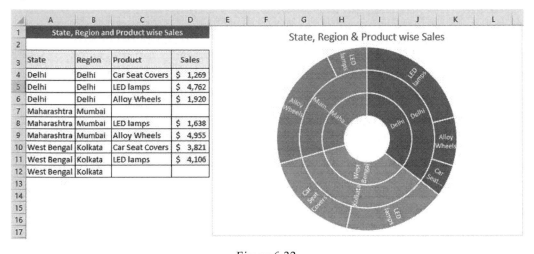

Figure 6.32

The outer circle for Maharashtra and West Bengal has only two categories, whereas that for Delhi has three.

Note: This chart type doesn't have sub-categories.

Histogram charts (only Office 2016 and above)

A Histogram chart is used to show the frequencies within a distribution. Each column in a histogram is like a bucket and can be edited too.

Let's take an example of a list of student and their scores. See the following *Figure 6.33*:

	A	B
1	**Student wise scores**	
2		
3	Student	Scores
4	Arjun	55
5	Deepak	26
6	Anuj	69
7	Devaang	82
8	Sunil	45
9	Alia	57
10	Mukesh	45
11	Ramakrishna	72
12	Divya	89
13	Keshav	25
14	Kunal	91
15	Vijya	18
16	Mukesh	78
17	Naveen	43
18	Rishi	91
19	Baldev	33

Figure 6.33

Insert a histogram chart by selecting the preceding data. See the following *Figure 6.34*:

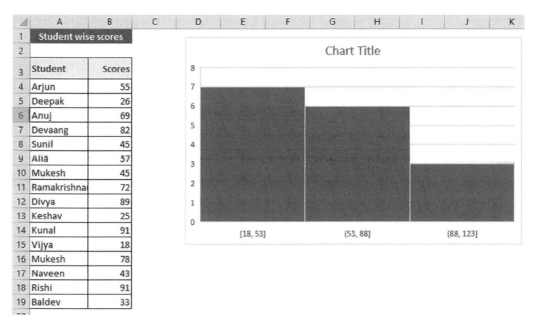

Figure 6.34

Initially the chart will form default bins for each column but the same can be edited as per your preference. To do so, double-click on the horizontal axis. This will open a format axis pane on the right. Edit the bins accordingly. For this example, change the bin width from default 35.0 to 15.0, and your final chart Should look as *Figure 6.35*:

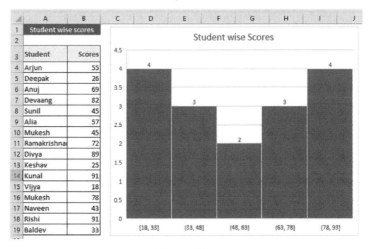

Figure 6.35

Refer the following *Table 6.9* for a brief understanding about the types of histogram charts:

Type of Histogram charts	Description
Histogram	It shows data in grouped bins.
Pareto Chart	It's a histogram chart where columns are stored in a descending order with a line representing the cumulative total percentage.

Waterfall chart (only Office 2016 and above)

A Waterfall chart shows the running totals of any financial data. In this chart it's easy to see how positive and negative values affect the initial value.

Let's consider an example of general home expenses and income and create a waterfall chart from it. See the following *Figure 6.36*:

	A	B
1	**Home Income & Expenses**	
2		
3	**Income/Expenses**	**Amount**
4	Salary (Income)	$ 10,000
5	Electricity	$ -800
6	Water	$ -450
7	Grocery	$ -1,200
8	Bank Interest	$ 1,590
9	Cable TV	$ -365
10	Mobile Ph. Bill	$ -285
11	Car Expenses	$ -490
12	Other Income	$ 800
13	Entertainment Exp.	$ -790
14	Misc. Exp.	$ -500
15	Total	$ 7,510

Figure 6.36

The Waterfall chart based on the preceding positive and negative values will be as follows. See the following *Figure 6.37*:

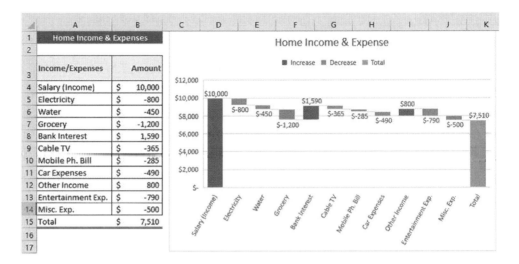

This chart type doesn't have sub-categories.

Combo charts (only Office 2013 and above)

Combo charts is a combination of two or more chart types into one plot area. This chart type is suitable for varied sets of data. Let's create a Combo chart based on the previous example of product-wise sales and number of units sold. See the following *Figure 6.38*:

Product	Sales	Units Sold
Car Seat Covers	$ 4,050	19
LED lamps	$ 2,978	9
Outer Graphics	$ 4,952	11
Upgraded Bumper	$ 1,413	12
Alloy Wheels	$ 3,260	16
Total	$ 16,653	67

Figure 6.38

As it isnot possible to show both the data series on the same axis, we will use the following Combo chart type: Clustered Column - Line on secondary axis. Here, columns represent sales data (which is plotted on primary vertical axis) and line represents the number of units sold (which is plotted on secondary vertical axis). See the following *Figure 6.39*:

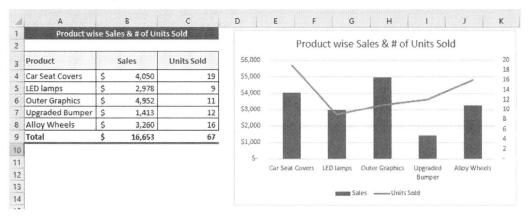

Figure 6.39

Pivot Charts

A pivot chart shows a pivot table data in the form of a chart. Here the pivot chart is connected to pivot table and slicer (optional).

Exercise file

A workbook containing the exercise files used in this chapter for Pivot Chart in Excel, is available on https://rebrand.ly/ffdbc, the file is named 6.2 Pivot Chart.xlsx. You can download it and practice along.

Exercise File: A workbook containing the exercise files used in this section for pivot charts is available on .... The file is named 6.2 Pivot Chart.xlsx. You can download it and practice along.

You can insert a pivot chart directly or you can insert it from the pivot table. Here, let's take the same sample data set we used for understanding pivot tables in the previous section. See the following *Figure 6.40*):

	A	B	C	D	E	F	G	H	I	J	K	L
1	Row	Order ID	Order Da	Ship Dat	Ship Mo	Customer	Customer Nan	Segme	Count	Ci	Sta	Postal
2	1	CA-2016-152156	08-11-2016	11-11-2016	Second Cla	CG-12520	Claire Gute	Consume	United S	Hen	Kentu	
3	2	CA-2016-152156	08-11-2016	11-11-2016	Second Cla	CG-12520	Claire Gute	Consume	United S	Hen	Kentu	
4	3	CA-2016-138688	12-06-2016	16-06-2016	Second Cla	DV-13045	Darrin Van Huff	Corporate	United S	Los A	Califo	
5	4	US-2015-108966	11-10-2015	18-10-2015	Standard Cl	SO-20335	Sean O'Donnell	Consume	United S	Fort	Florid	
6	5	US-2015-108966	11-10-2015	18-10-2015	Standard Cl	SO-20335	Sean O'Donnell	Consume	United S	Fort	Florid	
7	6	CA-2014-115812	09-06-2014	14-06-2014	Standard Cl	BH-11710	Brosina Hoffman	Consume	United S	Los A	Califo	
8	7	CA-2014-115812	09-06-2014	14-06-2014	Standard Cl	BH-11710	Brosina Hoffman	Consume	United S	Los A	Califo	
9	8	CA-2014-115812	09-06-2014	14-06-2014	Standard Cl	BH-11710	Brosina Hoffman	Consume	United S	Los A	Califo	
10	9	CA-2014-115812	09-06-2014	14-06-2014	Standard Cl	BH-11710	Brosina Hoffman	Consume	United S	Los A	Califo	
11	10	CA-2014-115812	09-06-2014	14-06-2014	Standard Cl	BH-11710	Brosina Hoffman	Consume	United S	Los A	Califo	
12	11	CA-2014-115812	09-06-2014	14-06-2014	Standard Cl	BH-11710	Brosina Hoffman	Consume	United S	Los A	Califo	
13	12	CA-2014-115812	09-06-2014	14-06-2014	Standard Cl	BH-11710	Brosina Hoffman	Consume	United S	Los A	Califo	
14	13	CA-2017-114412	15-04-2017	20-04-2017	Standard Cl	AA-10480	Andrew Allen	Consume	United S	Conc	North	
15	14	CA-2016-161389	05-12-2016	10-12-2016	Standard Cl	IM-15070	Irene Maddox	Consume	United S	Seat	Wash	
16	15	US-2015-118983	22-11-2015	26-11-2015	Standard Cl	HP-14815	Harold Pawlan	Home Off	United S	Fort	Texas	
17	16	US-2015-118983	22-11-2015	26-11-2015	Standard Cl	HP-14815	Harold Pawlan	Home Off	United S	Fort	Texas	

Figure 6.40

To create a pivot chart directly, follow the steps:

1. Select the complete data including headers.

2. Under the Insert tab select PivotChart.

3. Here you can either choose to insert it into a new worksheet or into an existing worksheet. For now, select the New worksheet option.

4. Click Ok.

See the following *Figure 6.41*:

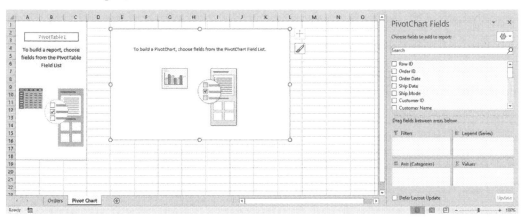

Figure 6.41

You will have both the pivot table and the pivot chart. On the right side of the screen, you have Pivot Chart Fields list. Let's try this chart for region- and segment-wise total sales. Drag the Region field and drop it into the Axis (Categories) box, the Segment field into the Legend (Series) box, and the Sales field into the Values box. See the following *Figure 6.42*:

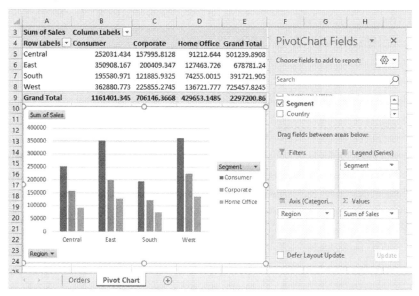

Figure 6.42

In addition to a usual chart, a pivot chart has field buttons. See the following *Figure 6.43*:

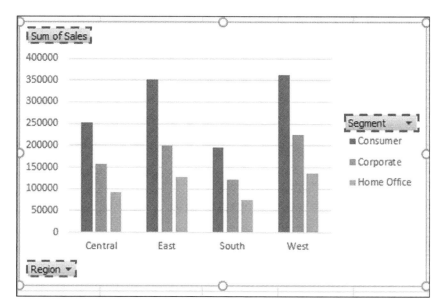

Figure 6.43

These field buttons help in filtering the data inside the chart directly. For example, let's select Consumer from the Segment field button drop-down. See the change in the following *Figure 6.44*:

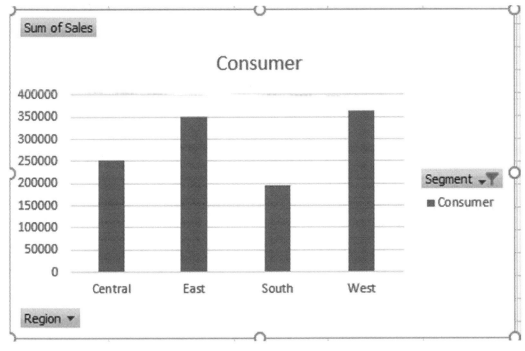

Figure 6.44

To create a pivot chart from the pivot table, follow the steps:

1. Place the cursor inside the existing pivot table.
2. Under the **Analyze** tab, go to the **Tools** group and select **Pivot Chart**.
3. Select the chart type.
4. Click **Ok**.

Slicer

A Slicer helps in filtering a pivot table or/and pivot chart. It works just like a report filter but is visually attractive and easy to use. The best part is that you can filter multiple pivottables with a single click of the slicer.

Exercise file

A workbook containing the exercise files used in this chapter for Slicers in Excel, is available on https://rebrand.ly/ffdbc, the file is named 6.3 Slicers & Timelines.xlsx. You can download it and practice along.

How to insert a Slicer

Follow the below steps to insert a Slicer.

1. Keep your cursor in the Pivot table area to keep it activated.
2. Under the Analyze tab, go to the Filters group and select Slicer.
3. Select the field(s) on which you need to apply the slicer.
4. Click Ok.

In Figure 6.45 shown below, a slicer is inserted based on the pivot chart example and the Category field is selected:

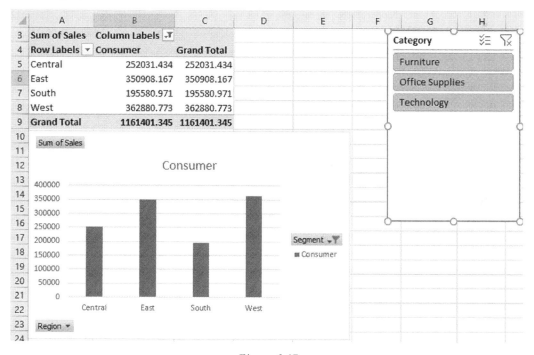

Figure 6.45

Here you can select the category you want to filter your pivot table and PivotChart on. You can also select multiple categories by either holding the *Ctrl* key and clicking on the categories you need or go to the Options tab in the Slicer Tools header.

Slicer options

Once a Slicer is inserted, the tab group Slicer Tools having only one tab, as Options is opened see the following *Figure 6.46*:

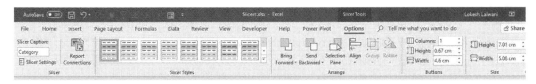

Figure 6.46

Here you can change several aspects of this slicer, such as name of the slicer, slicer style, establishing connection with other pivot table reports, arranging it with other slicers or objects, increasing the number of columns (if the list of items in a slicer is huge), and adjusting the height and width of the slicer.

Of the preceding options, Report Connections option is worth discussing. Through this you can connect multiple pivot tables. When there are multiple pivot tables in the current workbook, Excel will show the complete list in the Report Connections option where you can choose the pivot table you want to connect to your Slicer. Suppose you have two different pivot table in your current workbook. Clicking on the Report Connections option will trigger a Report Connections dialogue box. Here, the one that is already checked indicates the pivot table from which you have inserted the slicer. Now if you check the other pivot tables, those will also get connected, and selecting any item from the slicer will make an impact on all the pivot tables. See the following *Figure 6.47*:

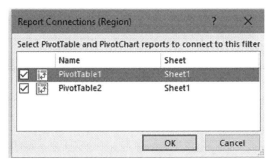

Figure 6.47

Slicer Settings

Apart from the general features of a Slicer available under the Options tab, you can also change other settings such as turning On or Off the headers; sorting the list of items in the slicer in ascending, descending, or customized order; hiding items; and showing or hiding items that have been removed from the data source. Just right-click on the slicer and select the option you want to change the setting for. See the following *Figure 6.48*:

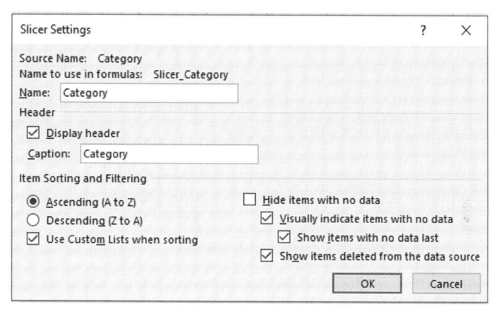

Figure 6.48

Timeline

A timeline is used to filter data on the basis of date. The look and feel of a timeline are the same as that of a slicer, and it can handle years of data so gracefully that Excel users just love this feature. With the help of this feature, you can easily filter your date -based data according to days, months, quarters, or even years.

Exercise file

A workbook containing the exercise files used in this chapter for Timeline in Excel, is available on https://rebrand.ly/ffdbc, the file is named 6.3 Slicers & Timelines.xlsx. You can download it and practice along.

How to insert a timeline

Let's take the same data set we used in the previous example and add a timeline to it based on Order Date or Ship Date. To insert a timeline follow the steps:

1. Keep your cursor in the pivot table area to keep it activated.

2. Under the Analyze tab, go to the Filters group and select Insert Timeline.

3. Select the field(s) for which you need the timeline (for example, Order Date).

4. Click Ok.

(See the following *Figure 6.49*):

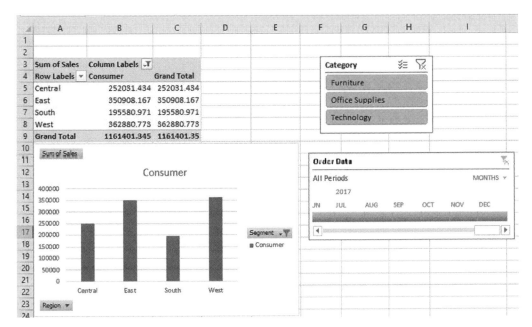

Figure 6.49

By default, this timeline shows a monthly view. You can change the same to yearly, Quarterly, monthly or daily view. See the following *Figure 6.50*:

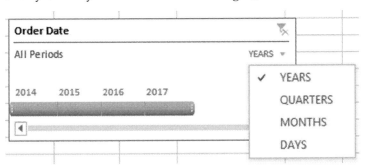

Figure 6.50

Clicking on the following bar will filter the data accordingly.

Timeline options

Figure 6.51

Here you can change several aspects of this timeline, such as name of the timeline, timeline style, establishing connection with other pivot table reports, arranging it with other timelines or objects, and adjusting the Height and Width of the timeline.

Few other relevant features found under the Options tab are turning On or Off the Header, Scrollbar, Selection Label, and Time Level. See the following *Figure 6.52*:

Figure 6.52

Sparklines

Sparklines are small charts that reside within a cell of an Excel worksheet. These are useful when you need a quick overview of the data without sparing the usual chart space. While these are small they are still these are very easy to read. Here you can even highlight the high and low points of the data too. Negative data points can also be highlighted very well. All in all, it offers a quick peek to any Excel user.

Three types of sparklines are available in Excel.

1. Line
2. Column
3. Win/Loss

Exercise file

A workbook containing the exercise files used in this chapter for Sparklines in Excel, is available on https://rebrand.ly/ffdbc, the file is named 6.4 Sparklines.xlsx. You can download it and practice along.

How to insert a sparkline

Let's understand this with the most common type of sparkline, that is, Line. This will create a line showing the trend of the selected range. Here you can additionally show the high point, low points, opening point and closing point as markers. You can create a Line Sparkline for a single data row and then drag it to apply it further for all the data rows.

For example, consider the Product wise Monthly Sales for nine months. See the following *Figure 6.53*:

	A	B	C	D	E	F	G	H	I	J
1	Product wise Monthly Sales									
2										
3	Product	Jan	Feb	Mar	Apr	May	Jun	Jul	Aug	Sep
4	Car Seat Covers	$584	$379	$891	$601	$338	$526	$848	$589	$458
5	LED lamps	$148	$850	$399	$278	$141	$394	$851	$918	$786
6	Outer Graphics	$231	$320	$923	$243	$607	$239	$552	$838	$334
7	Upgraded Bumper	$275	$937	$462	$695	$609	$559	$609	$950	$367
8	Alloy Wheels	$768	$837	$516	$484	$406	$720	$467	$185	$921

Figure 6.53

Follow the steps to insert Line Sparkline:

1. Activate the cell where you want to have a Sparkline (for example, cell K4).

2. Under the Insert tab, select the Sparklines group and then select Line. (This will trigger a dialogue box).

3. Select Data Range for which you want to create the sparkline (for example, B4:J4).

4. **Location Range** will be set to k4 (it's already selected in *Step 1*, that is, K4).

(See the following *Figure 6.54*):

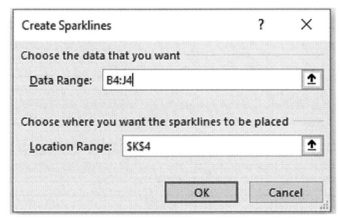

Figure 6.54

5. Click Ok.

This will insert a Sparkline for the selected data range only. For the rest of the ranges, that is, products, just drag the cell down and a copy of the same will be created with modified range. See the following *Figure 6.55*:

⟋	A	B	C	D	E	F	G	H	I	J	K
1				Product wise Monthly Sales							
2											
3	Product	Jan	Feb	Mar	Apr	May	Jun	Jul	Aug	Sep	
4	Car Seat Covers	$584	$379	$891	$601	$338	$526	$848	$589	$458	
5	LED lamps	$148	$850	$399	$278	$141	$394	$851	$918	$786	
6	Outer Graphics	$231	$320	$923	$243	$607	$239	$552	$838	$334	
7	Upgraded Bumper	$275	$937	$462	$695	$609	$559	$609	$950	$367	
8	Alloy Wheels	$768	$837	$516	$484	$406	$720	$467	$185	$921	

Figure 6.55

You can increase the column width to have a good look at the Sparklines.

The process is the same for Column and Win/Loss Sparklines.

Highlighting points in Sparklines

Sparklines offer an amazing option to highlight important points such as High, Low, First, Last, Negative, and so on This is a very user-friendly feature as, along with the trend it shows the most important points related to the data and make it more meaningful.

To show these important points on a line, keep the sparklines selected and go to the Design tab. Under Sparkline Tools in the ribbon, select the Show group and check the boxes relevant to your data, for example, Show high point and low point. The result will look as *Figure 6.56*:

⟋	A	B	C	D	E	F	G	H	I	J	K
1				Product wise Monthly Sales							
2											
3	Product	Jan	Feb	Mar	Apr	May	Jun	Jul	Aug	Sep	
4	Car Seat Covers	$584	$379	$891	$601	$338	$526	$848	$589	$458	
5	LED lamps	$148	$850	$399	$278	$141	$394	$851	$918	$786	
6	Outer Graphics	$231	$320	$923	$243	$607	$239	$552	$838	$334	
7	Upgraded Bumper	$275	$937	$462	$695	$609	$559	$609	$950	$367	
8	Alloy Wheels	$768	$837	$516	$484	$406	$720	$467	$185	$921	

Figure 6.56

Sparkline styles

You are not bound to use the default sparkline style every time. Excel provides decent number of styles to choose from. To do so, select the cell with the sparkline. Then under the Design tab, select Sparkline Tools in the ribbon and then select the

Style group. Expand this group to choose the one you want. Select the same and you are done. See the following *Figure 6.57*:

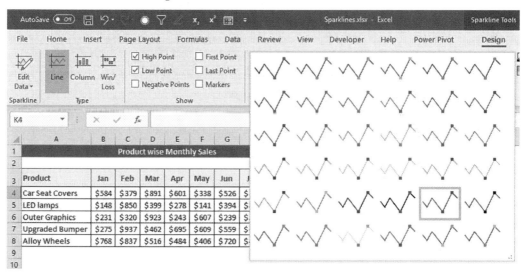

Figure 6.57

Handle empty or hidden cells

Sparkline also gives the option to handle any empty or hidden cell present in the data range. If a cell is empty or hidden, then by default Excel will show a break in the Sparkline. This can be managed with several options. Let's use the earlier sample data set but with some empty cells. See the following *Figure 6.58*:

	A	B	C	D	E	F	G	H	I	J
1	Product wise Monthly Sales									
2										
3	Product	Jan	Feb	Mar	Apr	May	Jun	Jul	Aug	Sep
4	Car Seat Covers	$584	$379		$601	$338		$848	$589	$458
5	LED lamps	$148	$850	$399	$278		$394	$851	$918	$786
6	Outer Graphics	$231	$320	$923	$243	$607	$239		$838	$334
7	Upgraded Bumper	$275	$937	$462		$609	$559	$609	$950	$367
8	Alloy Wheels	$768	$837	$516	$484	$406		$467	$185	$921

Figure 6.58

Let's insert a Sparkline and see how it looks like by default. See the following *Figure 6.59*:

▲	A	B	C	D	E	F	G	H	I	J	K
1				Product wise Monthly Sales							
2											
3	Product	Jan	Feb	Mar	Apr	May	Jun	Jul	Aug	Sep	
4	Car Seat Covers	$584	$379		$601	$338		$848	$589	$458	
5	LED lamps	$148	$850	$399	$278		$394	$851	$918	$786	
6	Outer Graphics	$231	$320	$923	$243	$607	$239		$838	$334	
7	Upgraded Bumper	$275	$937	$462		$609	$559	$609	$950	$367	
8	Alloy Wheels	$768	$837	$516	$484	$406		$467	$185	$921	

Figure 6.59

Breaks are clearly visible in the preceding figure.

To manage the empty cells, go to the Design tab and under Sparkline Tools in the ribbon select the Sparkline group. Then click on the Edit Data dropdown icon and select Hidden & Empty cells. This will trigger a dialogue box with few options where you can select Gaps, which is already selected, or you can select Zero (this will just drop the line to bottom) or Connect data points with line (this will join the gaps with a line).

As of now let's go with the last option, that is, Connect data points with line. See the following *Figure 6.60*:

▲	A	B	C	D	E	F	G	H	I	J	K
1				Product wise Monthly Sales							
2											
3	Product	Jan	Feb	Mar	Apr	May	Jun	Jul	Aug	Sep	
4	Car Seat Covers	$584	$379		$601	$338		$848	$589	$458	
5	LED lamps	$148	$850	$399	$278		$394	$851	$918	$786	
6	Outer Graphics	$231	$320	$923	$243	$607	$239		$838	$334	
7	Upgraded Bumper	$275	$937	$462		$609	$559	$609	$950	$367	
8	Alloy Wheels	$768	$837	$516	$484	$406		$467	$185	$921	

Figure 6.60

Conditional Formatting (CF)

Since ages, conditional formatting has been one of the most admired visualization tools. It helps is formatting the cells on the basis of certain conditions, for example, highlighting cells if the values go above or below a certain level, highlighting top five or bottom ten values, highlighting duplicate values, and so on. You can also add color bars and icons based on the values in the range. If all this still does not satisfy your visual conditional needs, then you can write your own functions to create customized conditions and format the cells accordingly. Let's dive into these amazing features.

Exercise File: A workbook containing the exercise files used in this section for conditional formatting, is available on .... The file is named 6.5 Conditional Formatting.xlsx. You can download it and practice along.

Exercise file

A workbook containing the exercise files used in this chapter for Conditional Formatting in Excel, is available on https://rebrand.ly/ffdbc, the file is named 6.5 Conditional Formatting.xlsx. You can download it and practice along.

Types of CF rules

There are several rules for Conditional Formatting. Let's explore them one by one and understand where we can use them.

Highlight cells rules

Under this bucket, you can highlight cells on the basis of conditions such as Greater Than..., Less Than..., Between..., Equal To..., A Date Occuring..., Text that Contains... something or duplicate values. Let's take a sample data set of Product category-wise sales. See the following *Figure 6.61*:

	A	B
1	Category wise Sales	
2		
3	Category	Sales
4	Bookcases	$ 821
5	Chairs	$ 2,107
6	Labels	$ 1,123
7	Tables	$ 777
8	Storage	$ 1,362
9	Furnishings	$ 897
10	Art	$ 1,917
11	Phones	$ 515
12	Binders	$ 1,078
13	Notepads	$ 537

Figure 6.61

Greater Than.../Less Than...

Suppose you want to highlight all the cells with sales value "Greater than" $1,000. To do so, select the sales values range, that is, B4:B13. Then go to the Home tab, select the Styles group, then Conditional Formatting, then Highlight Cells Rules, and finally Greater than.... Dialogue box will pop-up, where you can write 1000. This will auto highlight the matching cells with pink color. You can choose your preferred colour from the drop-down on the right side of the box and choose Custom Format. This will further pop-up a dialogue box (as shown in the following *Figure 6.62*):

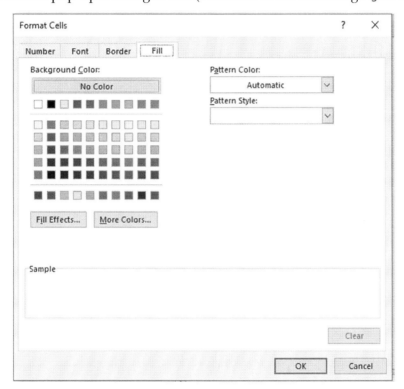

Figure 6.62

Here, you can go to the Fill tab and select a colour. Then click Ok.

This will highlight all the sales values that are more than $1000. See the following *Figure 6.63*:

	A	B
1	Category wise Sales	
2		
3	Category	Sales
4	Bookcases	$ 821
5	Chairs	$ 2,107
6	Labels	$ 1,123
7	Tables	$ 777
8	Storage	$ 1,362
9	Furnishings	$ 897
10	Art	$ 1,917
11	Phones	$ 515
12	Binders	$ 1,078
13	Notepads	$ 537

Figure 6.63

Follow the same procedure for the Less than… case.

Between…/Equal To…

Suppose in the preceding sample data set you want to highlight all values between $1,000 and $1,500. To highlight the required values, select the same and go to the Home tab. Under the Styles group, select Conditional Formatting, then Highlight Cells Rules, and select Between…. This will trigger a dialogue box. Fill in the respective values, i.e., $1,000 and $1,500, and choose the desired color. See the following *Figure 6.64*:

Figure 6.64

Clicking Ok will give you the result as shown in the following *Figure 6.65*:

	A	B
1	Category wise Sales	
2		
3	Category	Sales
4	Bookcases	$ 821
5	Chairs	$ 2,107
6	Labels	$ 1,123
7	Tables	$ 777
8	Storage	$ 1,362
9	Furnishings	$ 897
10	Art	$ 1,917
11	Phones	$ 515
12	Binders	$ 1,078
13	Notepads	$ 537

Figure 6.65

Follow the same procedure for the Equal To... case.

Text that Contains...

This Conditional Formatting rule highlights all cells having some text that matches with the given condition. For example, consider a list of companies where you want to highlight all TATA group companies, i.e., having TATA as the common text. See the following *Figure 6.66*:

Figure 6.66

To perform the task, select all the company names and go to the Home tab. Under the Styles group, select Conditional Formatting, then Highlight Cells Rules, and finally select Text that Contains…. Type tata and choose your preferred color. See the following *Figure 6.67*:

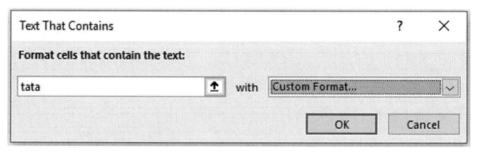

Figure 6.67

Click Ok and you'll see the result as shown in the following *Figure 6.68*:

	A	
1	**List of Top Companies**	
2		
3	Companies	
4	Tata Communications	
5	Tata Sky	
6	Sun Pharmaceutical	
7	Tata Consultancy Services	
8	Sterlite Industries	
9	Royal Enfield	
10	Tata Motors	
11	Tata Steel	
12	Myntra	
13	Rupani Footwear	
14	Tata Chemicals	
15	Tata Technologies	
16	Muthoot	

Figure 6.68

A Date Occurring...

Using this option, you can create any suitable condition related to dates, e.g., highlighting a date throughout the data set or perhaps last/this/next week's dates, etc. Consider a hotel's database containing date-wise customer complaints, and you want to highlight only the current month's complaints.

Note: This is a dynamic condition, so this feature will consider only those cells that fall within last 7 days from the current system date.

See the following *Figure 6.69*:

◢	A	B
1	Date wise Customer Complaints	
2		
3	Date	Complaint type
4	10-02-2019	Rude Staff
5	12-02-2019	No Hot Water
6	20-02-2019	Rude Staff
7	28-02-2019	Bad Food
8	15-03-2019	Unclean Rooms
9	16-03-2019	Rude Staff
10	18-03-2019	Uncomfortable Rooms
11	19-03-2019	Bad Food
12	20-03-2019	Unclean Rooms
13	23-03-2019	Rude Staff

Figure 6.69

Follow the same steps as those for conditional formatting, but this time go with A Date Occurring…. From the drop-down list in the dialog box choose, in the last 7 days and choose your preferred color. See the following *Figure 6.70*:

◢	A	B
1	**Date wise Customer Complaints**	
2		
3	Date	Complaint type
4	10-02-2019	Rude Staff
5	12-02-2019	No Hot Water
6	20-02-2019	Rude Staff
7	28-02-2019	Bad Food
8	15-03-2019	Unclean Rooms
9	16-03-2019	Rude Staff
10	18-03-2019	Uncomfortable Rooms
11	19-03-2019	Bad Food
12	20-03-2019	Unclean Rooms
13	23-03-2019	Rude Staff

Figure 6.70

Duplicate Values…

This option highlights all the cells having duplicate values in the selected range. Let's take a sample data set of employee IDs of a company where they want to give some benefits to certain employees. They want to avoid duplicate entries of any employee ID so that they do not end up giving the benefits multiple times to a single employee. As the Emp. ID is unique, they can apply the Duplicate values formatting on Emp. ID. See the following *Figure 6.71*:

	A	B
1	Employee Data	
2		
3	Emp. ID	Region
4	CG-12520	South
5	DV-13045	West
6	SO-20335	Central
7	BH-11710	North
8	AA-10480	West
9	IM-15070	North
10	HP-14815	North
11	PK-19075	North
12	SO-20335	Central
13	ZD-21925	South
14	KB-16585	North
15	SF-20065	South
16	EB-13870	South
17	IM-15070	North
18	TB-21520	West
19	MA-17560	West

Figure 6.71

You can choose to highlight unique values instead of duplicate values). Select the preferred color, and click Ok. See the following *Figure 6.72*:

	A	B
1	**Employee Data**	
2		
3	Emp. ID	Region
4	CG-12520	South
5	DV-13045	West
6	SO-20335	Central
7	BH-11710	North
8	AA-10480	West
9	IM-15070	North
10	HP-14815	North
11	PK-19075	North
12	SO-20335	Central
13	ZD-21925	South
14	KB-16585	North
15	SF-20065	South
16	EB-13870	South
17	IM-15070	North
18	TB-21520	West
19	MA-17560	West

Figure 6.72

Top/Bottom rules

Using this rule, you can highlight the top or bottom values, top or bottom n % values, above or below average values, and so on. It helps to quickly visualize key values in a huge set of data. This is immensely useful for almost any department of a company. Let's understand the broad category of conditions available under this rule.

Top/Bottom n values

Suppose you have the sales data for different product categories over a given period and want to highlight the top or bottom n sales values. See the following *Figure 6.73*:

	A	B
1	Category wise Sales	
2		
3	Category	Sales
4	Bookcases	$ 821
5	Chairs	$ 2,107
6	Labels	$ 1,123
7	Tables	$ 777
8	Storage	$ 1,362
9	Furnishings	$ 897
10	Art	$ 1,917
11	Phones	$ 515
12	Binders	$ 1,078
13	Notepads	$ 537

Figure 6.73

Select all the categories and go to the Home tab. Under the Styles group, select Conditional Formatting, then Top/Bottom Rules,and finally Top 10 Items.... type 5 for the top 5 values and select the preferred color. See the following *Figure 6.74*:

	A	B
1	Category wise Sales	
2		
3	Category	Sales
4	Bookcases	$ 821
5	Chairs	$ 2,107
6	Labels	$ 1,123
7	Tables	$ 777
8	Storage	$ 1,362
9	Furnishings	$ 897
10	Art	$ 1,917
11	Phones	$ 515
12	Binders	$ 1,078
13	Notepads	$ 537

Figure 6.74

Top/Bottom n % values

Using this, you can highlight the top/bottom *n* % values from the data. For example, let's take the same sample data set we used above and highlight the Top 25% values. To do so, go to the Home tab and select the Styles group. Select Conditional Formatting, then Top/Bottom Rules, and finally Top 10 %…. Type 25 in the % box and choose the preferred color, and click Ok. See the following *Figure 6.75*:

⬀	A	B
1	Category wise Sales	
2		
3	Category	Sales
4	Bookcases	$ 821
5	Chairs	$ 2,107
6	Labels	$ 1,123
7	Tables	$ 777
8	Storage	$ 1,362
9	Furnishings	$ 897
10	Art	$ 1,917
11	Phones	$ 515
12	Binders	$ 1,078
13	Notepads	$ 537

Figure 6.75

Above/Below Average values

It will calculate the average of all the selected cells and highlight cells accordingly. You can go with the above or the below average values. By taking the same sample data set, lets highlight the above average sales values. Go to the Home tab, a nd select the Styles group. Under Conditional Formatting, select Top/Bottom Rules, and then Above Average…. Choose the preferred color, and click Ok. See the following *Figure 6.76*:

◢	A	B
1	Category wise Sales	
2		
3	Category	Sales
4	Bookcases	$ 821
5	Chairs	$ 2,107
6	Labels	$ 1,123
7	Tables	$ 777
8	Storage	$ 1,362
9	Furnishings	$ 897
10	Art	$ 1,917
11	Phones	$ 515
12	Binders	$ 1,078
13	Notepads	$ 537

Figure 6.76

Data Bars

Data Bars are used to insert color bars in cells on the basis of values present in them. There are two options in Data Bars: Gradient Fill and Solid Fill. These are very useful in dashboard creation in Excel. Using the same sample data set, as above, let's apply data bars with gradient fill. To perform this task, select all sales value cells and go to the Home tab. Under the Styles group, select Conditional Formatting, then Data Bars, and finally Gradient Fill. Then and choose the preferred color. See the following *Figure 6.77*:

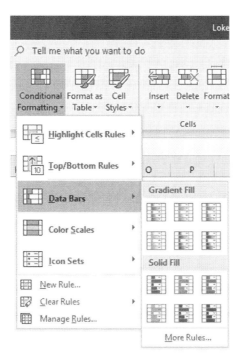

Figure 6.77

	A	B
1	**Category wise Sales**	
2		
3	**Category**	**Sales**
4	Bookcases	$ 821
5	Chairs	$ 2,107
6	Labels	$ 1,123
7	Tables	$ 777
8	Storage	$ 1,362
9	Furnishings	$ 897
10	Art	$ 1,917
11	Phones	$ 515
12	Binders	$ 1,078
13	Notepads	$ 537

Figure 6.78

In *Figure 6.78* above, you can see that the higher sales values have larger color bars as opposed to lower values. This helps the user to easily differentiate between higher and lower values.

Color scales

Color scales will fill the background of the cells with colors based on the values in the range. The shade of the color helps the user to visualize the data easily. Let's take an example of the number of defects in manufacturing products. You can set the color scales in such a way that the higher the number of defects the darker the colour of the cells (in red) and vice versa (in white). See the following *Figure 6.79*:

	A	B
1	Category wise number of defects	
2		
3	Category	Number of defects
4	Bookcases	47
5	Chairs	52
6	Labels	80
7	Tables	65
8	Storage	64
9	Furnishings	84
10	Art	17
11	Phones	86
12	Binders	17
13	Notepads	93

Figure 6.79

To apply color scales, select the range of cells having defects and go to the Home tab. Then in the **Styles** group, select **Conditional Formatting**, then **Color Scales**, and then choose the preferred one (that is, red - white color scale). See the following *Figure 6.80*:

	A	B
1	Category wise number of defects	
2		
3	Category	Number of defects
4	Bookcases	47
5	Chairs	52
6	Labels	80
7	Tables	65
8	Storage	64
9	Furnishings	84
10	Art	17
11	Phones	86
12	Binders	17
13	Notepads	93
14		

Figure 6.80

Icon sets

Using Icon Sets, you can display symbols in front of every value in a range to indicate its weight, within the complete range. Icon Sets include a bucket of symbols, as shown in the following *Figure 6.81*:

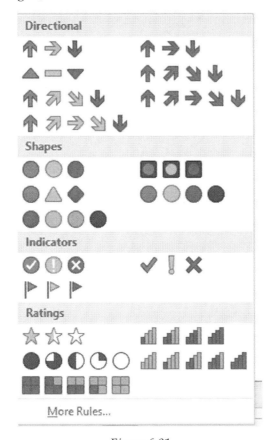

Figure 6.81

Let's take the same sample data set we used for Data Bars where we have a list of product categories and their amount of sales. You can apply three colored arrows. Go to the Home tab, and select the Styles group. Under Conditional Formatting, select Icon Sets, then Directional, and then 3 Arrows (Colored). See the following *Figure 6.82*:

	A	B
1	Category wise Sales	
2		
3	Category	Sales
4	Bookcases	$ 821
5	Chairs	$ 2,107
6	Labels	$ 1,123
7	Tables	$ 777
8	Storage	$ 1,362
9	Furnishings	$ 897
10	Art	$ 1,917
11	Phones	$ 515
12	Binders	$ 1,078
13	Notepads	$ 537

Figure 6.82

In the preceding example, conditional formatting has divided the data into three sections of 33.33% each. Higher 33.33% values in the range will get green-colored upward arrow, middle 33.33% values will get yellow-colored rightward arrow and finally lowest 33.33% values will get red colored downward arrow.

Conditional formatting based on formulas

Let's apply one more conditional formatting rule based on a formula. For example, you have a list of top Indian companies and want to highlight TATA and Reliance Group. See the following *Figure 6.83*:

	A	B
1		
2	List of Top Companies	
3	Tata Communications	Reliance Entertainment
4	Tata Sky	Indian Oil Corporation
5	Sun Pharmaceutical	State Bank of India
6	Tata Consultancy Services	Rajesh Exports
7	Sterlite Industries	Rupani Footwear
8	Royal Enfield	Reliance Infrastructure
9	Tata Motors	Tata Technologies
10	Tata Steel	Muthoot
11	Myntra	Reliance Communications
12	Tata Chemicals	Ador Group

Figure 6.83

To apply a formula-based conditional formatting rule, select the data and go to the Home tab. Under the Styles group, select Conditional Formatting and then New Rule….This will trigger a dialogue box. Next select Use a formula to determine which cells to format and insert the following formula as =OR(A3="TATA Group",A3="Reliance Group")

See the following *Figure 6.84*:

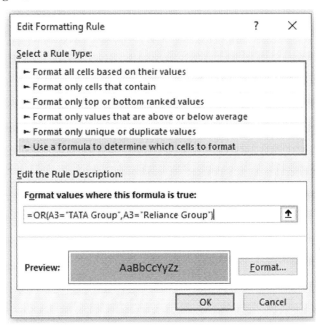

Figure 8.84

This will highlight cells having Tata Group and Reliance Group. See the following *Figure 8.85*:

2	List of Top Companies	
3	Muthoot	Reliance Group
4	ITC	Indian Oil Corporation
5	Sahara India Pariwar	State Bank of India
6	Aditya Birla Group	Rajesh Exports
7	Ador Group	Adani Group
8	Balaji Group	Arvind
9	Essar Group	Torrent Group
10	GVK	Vadilal
11	Myntra	United Breweries Group
12	Tata Group	Shriram Group

Figure 8.85

Clear conditional formatting rules

You can clear rules from the selected cells, entire sheet, from a table or a pivot table.

To clear a rule from the selected cells, select the respective cell and go to the **Home** tab. Then in the **Styles** group, select **Conditional Formatting**, then **Clear Rules**, and finally **Clear rules from Selected Cells**.

To **Clear Rules from Entire Sheet**, selection does not matter.

To **Clear Rules from This Table** or **Clear Rules from This PivotTable**, selection of the desired table is mandatory.

Power Map

Power map is a 3-dimensional data visualization tool. It helps in plotting geographical data on a globe. This helps in gaining insights from the data on a 3-D globe. This feature of Microsoft Excel uses Bing map engine and plots exact geographical locations.

Exercise file

A workbook containing the exercise files used in this chapter for Power Map in Excel, is available on https://rebrand.ly/ffdbc, the file is named 6.6 Power Map.xlsx. You can download it and practice along.

Let's take a sample data from food inspection conducted in Seattle and plot it on a power map. See the following *Figure 6.86*:

	A	B	C	D	E	F	G	H	I	J	K
1	Name	Program Identifier	Inspection Dat	Descrip	Addres	City	Zip Cod	Phone	Longitu	Latitud	Inspect
2	@ The PEAK	@ The PEAK	25-01-2013	Seating 13	401 BROA	SEATTLE	98122	(206) 947-	-122.321	47.60562	@ The P
3	@ The PEAK	@ The PEAK	25-01-2013	Seating 13	401 BROA	SEATTLE	98122	(206) 947-	-122.321	47.60562	@ The P
4	@ The PEAK	@ The PEAK	25-01-2013	Seating 13	401 BROA	SEATTLE	98122	(206) 947-	-122.321	47.60562	@ The P
5	@ The PEAK	@ The PEAK	25-01-2013	Seating 13	401 BROA	SEATTLE	98122	(206) 947-	-122.321	47.60562	@ The P
6	@ The PEAK	@ The PEAK	28-09-2012	Seating 13	401 BROA	SEATTLE	98122	(206) 947-	-122.321	47.60562	@ The P
7	@ The PEAK	@ The PEAK	02-05-2012	Seating 13	401 BROA	SEATTLE	98122	(206) 947-	-122.321	47.60562	@ The P
8	@ The PEAK	@ The PEAK	02-02-2012	Seating 13	401 BROA	SEATTLE	98122	(206) 947-	-122.321	47.60562	@ The P
9	@ The PEAK	@ The PEAK	02-02-2012	Seating 13	401 BROA	SEATTLE	98122	(206) 947-	-122.321	47.60562	@ The P
10	@ The PEAK	@ The PEAK	02-02-2012	Seating 13	401 BROA	SEATTLE	98122	(206) 947-	-122.321	47.60562	@ The P
11	@ The PEAK	@ The PEAK	29-09-2011	Seating 13	401 BROA	SEATTLE	98122	(206) 947-	-122.321	47.60562	@ The P
12	@ The PEAK	@ The PEAK	12-05-2011	Seating 13	401 BROA	SEATTLE	98122	(206) 947-	-122.321	47.60562	@ The P
13	@ The PEAK	@ The PEAK	12-05-2011	Seating 13	401 BROA	SEATTLE	98122	(206) 947-	-122.321	47.60562	@ The P
14	@ The PEAK	@ The PEAK	12-05-2011	Seating 13	401 BROA	SEATTLE	98122	(206) 947-	-122.321	47.60562	@ The P

Figure 6.86

To create a 3-D power map select the data and then go to the **Insert** tab. Select **Tours** group and then **3D Maps** (see the following *Figure 6.87*:

Figure 6.87

Excel will pop-up a dialog box to launch 3-D maps and will detect the geographical field automatically from the selected data. See the following *Figure 6.88*:

Launch 3D Maps   ✕

King County
Food
Inspection

 New Tour

Figure 6.88

By clicking on the thumbnail in the preceding figure, a 3-D map will be created, where you can choose from either a 3-D globe or a flat map.

A glimpse of a 3-D map can be seen in the following *Figure 6.89*:

Figure 6.89

You can use the curser to drag and move plot area in this chart to view different geographical locations.

Summary

The visualization features discussed here will help you provide a *wow* experience to your report consumers. Data visualization highlights details about the data that you would like to show them. Some of the options not discussed here are open for you to dig in and play around with your own creative mind in order to create something that will help the end user.

Next, it's time to discuss the data extraction techniques available in Excel, because ultimately, we need to serve this data either on a hard paper or through publishing. So, in the next chapter, we will be discussing the important methods used to extract data from Excel.

CHAPTER 7

Data Extraction

Once your data is visualized and analyzed, data extraction is the next step. Excel offers several ways to perform this task. In this chapter, we will discuss how to print a worksheet and how to handle the glitches encountered while printing. You will also learn how to set up pages for printing. Further, Excel 2019/Office 365 give us the option of publishing data to the Power BI platform, where you can use the immense power of this amazing business intelligence tool to create interactive dashboards.

Structure:

In this chapter, we will discuss:

- Print Excel files
- Export or upload data to Power BI
- Share files via email
- Export data in different file formats

Objective:

The objective of this chapter is to give you overall knowledge on how to extract the data you have analyzed and visualized. Excel provides several ways to extract data. Here you will understand how to print a worksheet's data. Although often it's pretty straight-forward, printing exactly what you want can become tricky. So, after going through this chapter, you will be able to print your worksheet's data accurately. You will also learn how to export or upload your data to the Power BI platform to create impressive dashboards. Finally, you will get a hold on how to share your files via email or export it in your desired format.

Print Excel Files

Although it's always good to save paper and avoid printing, at times it becomes next to impossible to do so. At such times, Excel printing options are of great help and work like a breeze. The printing options available in Excel are very easy to use and can help us immensely in putting professional reports on paper.

Exercise file

A workbook containing the exercise files used in this chapter for printing in Excel, is available on https://rebrand.ly/ffdbc, the file is named 7.1 Print in Excel.xlsx. You can download it and practice along.

Understanding page view

Page view plays an important role in printing a worksheet, and therefore it's better to understand this feature first to move forward in the world of printing.

Three different page views are available in Excel:

- Normal
- Page layout
- Page break preview

Let's understand them one by one.

Normal view

Normal view is a default view of an Excel worksheet. This is the view where you see cells with gridlines and do your work. In this view, you can also see the page break as dotted lines when you print or print preview the worksheet. These page breaks get adjusted automatically depending upon the change in the width and height of columns or rows, page orientation etc. Refer *Figure 7.1* to see how these page breaks in normal view:

de	Customer ID	Customer Name	Segment	Postal Co	Region	Product ID	Category
Class	CG-12520	Claire Gute	Consumer	42420	South	FUR-BO-10001798	Furniture
Class	CG-12520	Claire Gute	Consumer	42420	South	FUR-CH-10000454	Furniture
Class	DV-13045	Darrin Van Huff	Corporate	90036	West	OFF-LA-10000240	Office Supplies
d Class	SO-20335	Sean O'Donnell	Consumer	33311	South	FUR-TA-10000577	Furniture
d Class	SO-20335	Sean O'Donnell	Consumer	33311	South	OFF-ST-10000760	Office Supplies
d Class	BH-11710	Brosina Hoffman	Consumer	90032	West	FUR-FU-10001487	Furniture
d Class	BH-11710	Brosina Hoffman	Consumer	90032	West	OFF-AR-10002833	Office Supplies
d Class	BH-11710	Brosina Hoffman	Consumer	90032	West	TEC-PH-10002275	Technology
d Class	BH-11710	Brosina Hoffman	Consumer	90032	West	OFF-BI-10003910	Office Supplies
d Class	BH-11710	Brosina Hoffman	Consumer	90032	West	OFF-AP-10002892	Office Supplies
d Class	BH-11710	Brosina Hoffman	Consumer	90032	West	FUR-TA-10001539	Furniture
d Class	BH-11710	Brosina Hoffman	Consumer	90032	West	TEC-PH-10002033	Technology
d Class	AA-10480	Andrew Allen	Consumer	28027	South	OFF-PA-10002365	Office Supplies
d Class	IM-15070	Irene Maddox	Consumer	98103	West	OFF-BI-10003656	Office Supplies
d Class	HP-14815	Harold Pawlan	Home Office	76106	Central	OFF-AP-10002311	Office Supplies
d Class	HP-14815	Harold Pawlan	Home Office	76106	Central	OFF-BI-10000756	Office Supplies
d Class	PK-19075	Pete Kriz	Consumer	53711	Central	OFF-ST-10004186	Office Supplies
Class	AG-10270	Alejandro Grove	Consumer	84084	West	OFF-ST-10000107	Office Supplies
Class	ZD-21925	Zuschuss Donatelli	Consumer	94109	West	OFF-AR-10003056	Office Supplies
Class	ZD-21925	Zuschuss Donatelli	Consumer	94109	West	TEC-PH-10001949	Technology
Class	ZD-21925	Zuschuss Donatelli	Consumer	94109	West	OFF-BI-10002215	Office Supplies
d Class	KB-16585	Ken Black	Corporate	68025	Central	OFF-AR-10000246	Office Supplies

Figure 7.1

Page layout view

Page layout view is the most appropriate view when printing a worksheet. It's like working on an Excel sheet in a printing environment. You can zoom in and out to look at the multiple pages in a single view. Header and footer are also visible in this view and can be directly added here. See the following *Figure 7.2*:

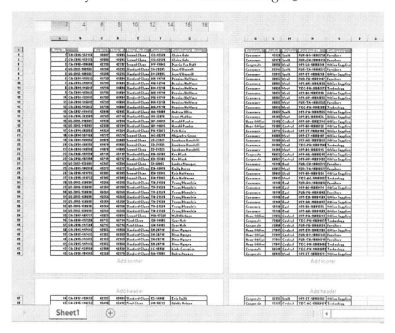

Figure 7.2

Page break preview

Page break preview shows the page breaks. These page breaks can be manually adjusted unlike normal view. Activating the page break preview will zoom out the sheet and accommodate more pages to see the page breaks. Also, the printing area comes with a white background and the non-printing will appear in grey. See the following *Figure 7.3*:

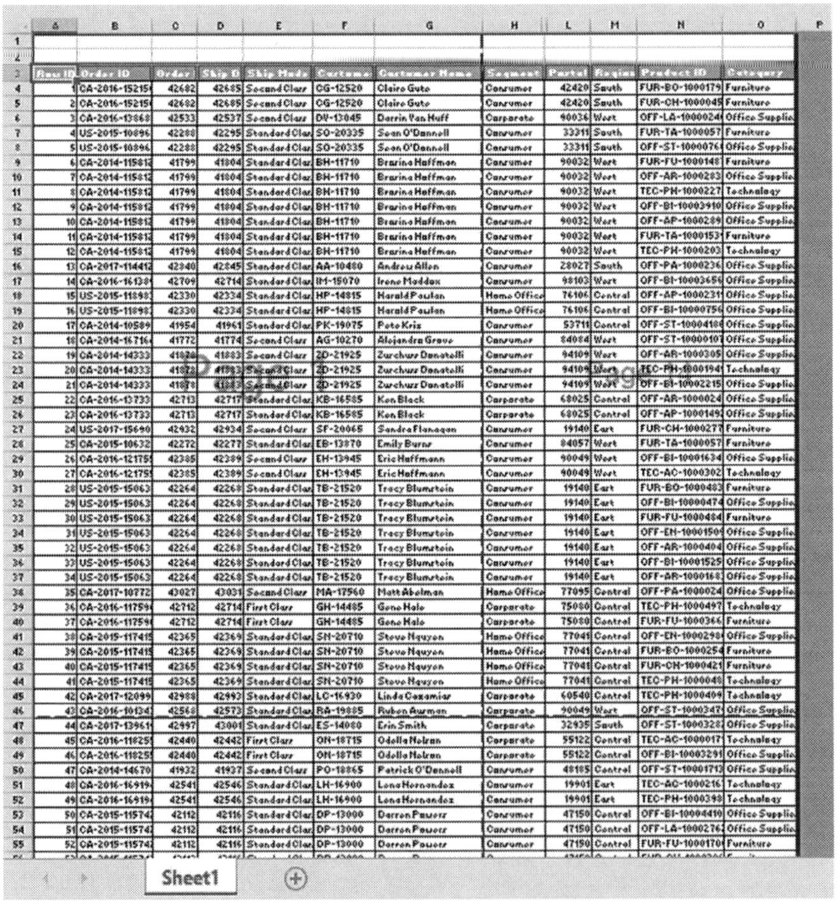

Figure 7.3

Understanding page setup options

Sometimes we need to modify the page settings of our Excel sheets to get them ready for printing. Also, there's an unsaid rule to keep your Excel sheets ready for printing before you share it with someone else. Let's review some of the most common page setup options used to make Excel files print-ready.

Setting print area

Suppose you want to print only a part of a sheet or only some of the pages from the complete data set. To facilitate this, Excel offers the following customized printing options.

- **Print Active Sheets**: This is the default printing option. This will print entire sheet. Even if multiple sheets are selected, all of them will get printed on separate pages.

- **Print Entire Workbook**: This will print the complete workbook.

- **Print Selection**: This will print only the selected part.

To choose from the preceding options, go to the **File** tab and **Print**. See the following *Figure 7.4*:

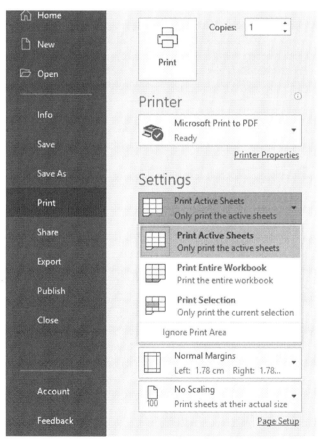

Figure 7.4

Page orientation

Using this option, you can either print the data as landscape or portrait. It completely depends on the layout of your data. If your data is huge in terms of rows and narrow in terms of columns, then you can go with Portrait Orientation (default page orientation) and if you have large number of columns then Landscape Orientation would be the preferred option.

These options can be found in the printing section, that is, Print under the File tab. See the following *Figure 7.5*:

Figure 7.5

Paper size

Although Excel offers many paper size options, an important point to remember is that not all printers support all paper sizes. You need to get familiar with your printer first. To check the paper size options, go to the File tab and select Print. See the following *Figure 7.6*:

Figure 7.6

Setting page margins

The unprinted area on each side of a page is known as margins. These are important to avoid any unwanted cutting in our printing data. You can have only one margin setting for all the pages that need to be printed at one go. When you turn on the Page Layout tab, rulers get activated by default. You can drag these to adjust the margin area.

To access margin settings, you can go to File tab select Print or Page Layout tab and then Margins. You'll see some pre-defined margin settings here. If you want different settings, you can go with Custom Margins. See the following *Figure 7.7*:

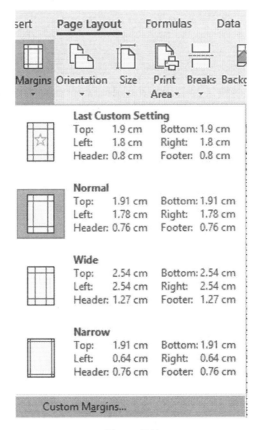

Figure 7.7

Printing report headers on each page

Headers and footers are the information we show on the top and bottom of each page respectively. By default, these are blank. You can add them by enabling Layout view and start typing headers and footers directly, or you can go to the Page Setup dialog box and set your headers and footers.

Headers and footers have three sections: Left, Center and Right. For example, you can show the page number on the left, workbook name in the center, and author name on the right.

You can also choose between pre-defined headers and footers and custom headers and footers, e.g., when you have several options such as inserting a file path or an image. You can further format the same too. (See the following *Figure 7.8*:

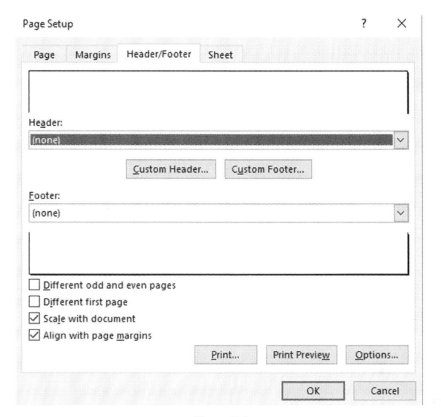

Figure 7.8

Printing report titles on each page

It's very common to have a long document or a table, where the field headers are mentioned on top of the data table. When such data is printed, field headers get printed only on the top and the reader must refer to the first page several times to get a hold on which column, on the rest of the pages, represents what. Now you can choose the header rows/columns that you want repeated on each page. To do so go to the Page Layout tab and select Print titles. Here you can select the rows and/or columns to be repeated on each page. See the following *Figure 7.9*:

Figure 7.9

Export or Upload to Power BI

Publishing to Power BI will help you create and share rich visual reports and dashboards from your workbook. Power BI offers two options:

1. Upload

2. Export

Upload

You can upload your Excel files directly to the Power BI environment. Here, you can interact with your Excel workbook in the same way you would in Excel online. Moreover, you can pin selected elements from your workbooks to Power BI dashboards and ultimately, you can share the elements of your workbook through Power BI.

Export

Using this option, you can export data from your Excel workbook to Power BI. From there, you can use this data to create data models and interactive dashboards.

See the following *Figure 7.10*:

Figure 7.10

Share files via Email

You can share your existing Excel workbook via email as an attachment in Excel or PDF format. This is probably the most common way of sharing an Excel file. For this go to the File tab and select Share. (See the following *Figure 7.11* and *Figure 7.12*:

Figure 7.11

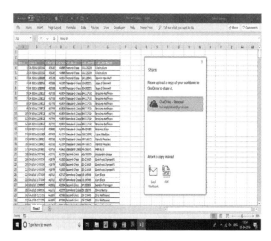

Figure 7.12

Export data in different file formats

You can export data from an Excel file in different file formats too. The list of file formats supported by Excel is given in the following *Figure 7.13*:

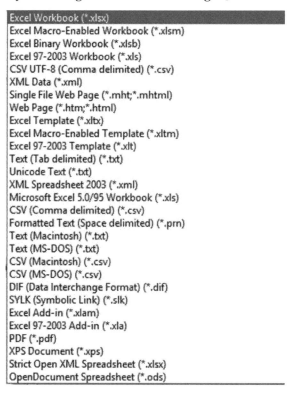

Figure 7.13

Summary

As you have seen, Excel offers some very useful data extraction options. Most of them can be used directly with a single click although in some cases customizations are required, (for example, while printing a worksheet, precise page setting is a key to perfect print). Also, uploading or exporting your data to the Power BI platform may be the preferred option when you want to create super-interactive dashboards in no time. Of course, you can also directly email your Excel files by sharing them as Excel or PDF. Further, you have the option to simply convert the file in your preferred format and then share it.

As we head towards the end of the book, it's important to know about "Macros". This is altogether a different planet in the solar system of Excel. Using macros you can automate the tasks you perform in Excel on a repetitive basis and let Excel do it for you in seconds.

CHAPTER 8

Automation in Excel through Macros

In this chapter, we will enter the world of automation. Automation of tasks can be done using VBA macros. Here you will learn what a Macro is and how to record and run a macro. Then we will investigate the code section of our recorded macro, and understand how to assign a macro to an object on a worksheet. Finally, you will learn how to edit or delete a macro. It is going to be a very interesting ride for you, so fasten your seatbelts!

Structure:

In this chapter, we will discuss about:

- Macros
- Difference between macros and VBA
- Record a Macro
- Save a Macro
- Run a Macro
- Assigning a macro to an object
- Check the VBA code
- Edit or delete a macro
- Macro security settings

Objective:

After going through this chapter, you will be able to record and run a macro. You will also be able to choose the right place to store a macro. Further, you will understand how to assign a macro to an object, for example, shapes. Also, you will be able to open **Visual Basic Editor** (**VBE**) and investigate the codes generated through macro recording. You will get a thorough understanding on how to edit or delete a macro. You'll get a quick look at the macro security settings.

Macros

The literal meaning of the word macro is—on a large scale. But do not confuse this with its meaning in Excel. Here, macro means to record your actions and play those recorded actions in future by hitting the specified keystroke on your keyboard or a toolbar button or an icon in a spreadsheet. Macros are mainly used when you have some repetitive work to perform in Excel. Suppose you want to prepare daily, weekly, bi-weekly, monthly, or quarterly reports, then while preparing that report for the first time you can simply start recording the macro when you prepare the report and after finishing the same, you can just stop the recording and you are done. So, in future, if you want to create that report again just hit the keystroke you assigned to that macro and Excel will take from few seconds to few minutes to prepare that report that would have taken you hours to create.

Difference between Macros and VBA

To know the difference between a macro and VBA, it's important to understand what VBA is. Whenever you record any task through Macro Recorder, Excel converts your actions into statements and saves it at the backstage of Excel. The language in which the statements are written is known as **Visual Basic for Applications** (**VBA**).

In short, a macro is a recorded program that uses VBA and on the other hand VBA is a language that Excel understand to perform tasks.

Now you may ask, if we can report easily, without going in to the technicality of the language, then do we need to understand or use VBA? The answer is yes, because programs recorded using Macro Recorder will record very straight forward programs, but using VBA you can create complex macros. Also, macros can be recorded only for something that already exists in Excel, for example, pivot table, charts, functions, etc., but any formula, function or feature which is unavailable in Excel, macros cannot be recorded but can be programmed using VBA. For example, you need to convert the salary amount mentioned in your Excel sheet into words so that you can print it on a bank cheque. Excel does not provide any function for this task, but you can surely write a code for the same suing VBA. Similarly, only Sub procedures can be recorded using "Macro Recorder" but using the "Sub" and "Function" procedures in VBA, both can be created. The list of differences between macros and VBA is huge. As a final note, you can see it as an iceberg, where a macro is the visible part, i.e., above water, and VBA is under water.

Record a macro

Before we proceed to understand how to record a macro, let's first discuss the ways through which we can record a macro. You can record a macro using any of the three ways mentioned as follows:

Developer tab

1. Go to File tab, select Options, and then select Customize Ribbon.

2. In the main tabs list under Customize Ribbon, check the Developer box and then click Ok.

View tab

1. Go to the View tab, select the Macros Group (extreme right), and choose Record Macros from the drop-down menu.

Status bar

1. Click on the Macro Recorder button on the status bar. See the following *Figure 8.1*:

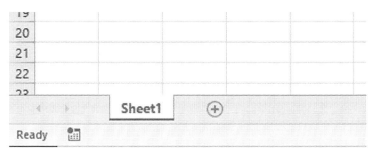

Figure 8.1

How to record a Macro

Let's take a real-world example to understand how and where we can use a macro. Suppose, your data set has some empty rows among the data and you need to delete those empty rows. To avoid doing it manually each time, you can record your steps the first time and then let Excel do the job for you thereafter. The sample data set has 550 plus rows as shown in the following *Figure 8.2*).

Exercise file

A workbook containing the exercise files used in this chapter for Automation through Macros in Excel, is available on https://rebrand.ly/ffdbc, the file is named

8.1 Automation through Macros.xlsm. You can download it and practice along.

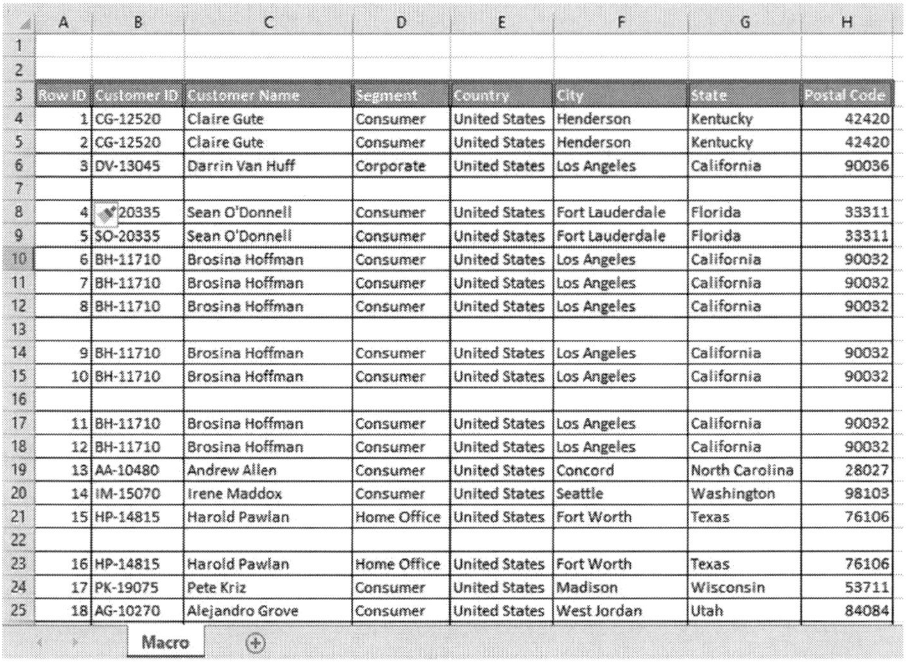

	A	B	C	D	E	F	G	H
1								
2								
3	Row ID	Customer ID	Customer Name	Segment	Country	City	State	Postal Code
4	1	CG-12520	Claire Gute	Consumer	United States	Henderson	Kentucky	42420
5	2	CG-12520	Claire Gute	Consumer	United States	Henderson	Kentucky	42420
6	3	DV-13045	Darrin Van Huff	Corporate	United States	Los Angeles	California	90036
7								
8	4	20335	Sean O'Donnell	Consumer	United States	Fort Lauderdale	Florida	33311
9	5	SO-20335	Sean O'Donnell	Consumer	United States	Fort Lauderdale	Florida	33311
10	6	BH-11710	Brosina Hoffman	Consumer	United States	Los Angeles	California	90032
11	7	BH-11710	Brosina Hoffman	Consumer	United States	Los Angeles	California	90032
12	8	BH-11710	Brosina Hoffman	Consumer	United States	Los Angeles	California	90032
13								
14	9	BH-11710	Brosina Hoffman	Consumer	United States	Los Angeles	California	90032
15	10	BH-11710	Brosina Hoffman	Consumer	United States	Los Angeles	California	90032
16								
17	11	BH-11710	Brosina Hoffman	Consumer	United States	Los Angeles	California	90032
18	12	BH-11710	Brosina Hoffman	Consumer	United States	Los Angeles	California	90032
19	13	AA-10480	Andrew Allen	Consumer	United States	Concord	North Carolina	28027
20	14	IM-15070	Irene Maddox	Consumer	United States	Seattle	Washington	98103
21	15	HP-14815	Harold Pawlan	Home Office	United States	Fort Worth	Texas	76106
22								
23	16	HP-14815	Harold Pawlan	Home Office	United States	Fort Worth	Texas	76106
24	17	PK-19075	Pete Kriz	Consumer	United States	Madison	Wisconsin	53711
25	18	AG-10270	Alejandro Grove	Consumer	United States	West Jordan	Utah	84084

Figure 8.2

To record a macro that will delete all the empty rows, follow the steps:

Select any of the preceding explained ways to record a macro, and then you will see a **Record Macro** dialog box on your screen. (see the following *Figure 8.3*):

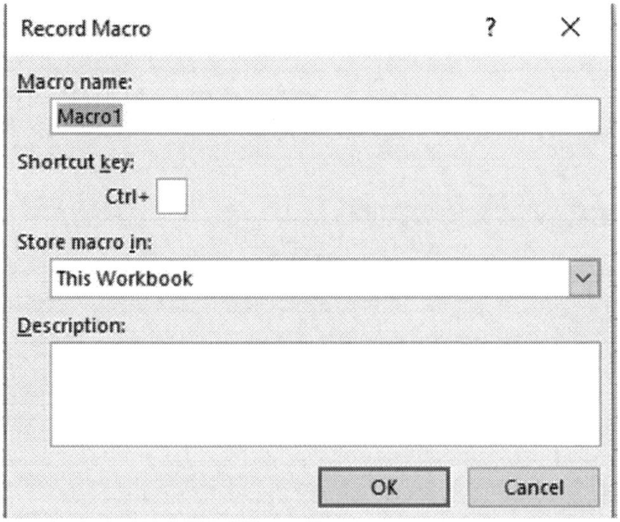

Figure 8.3

Name a macro

First thing required to fill in is the Macro name. But bear in mind the following few things that can't be accepted as part of a macro name:

- No spaces

- No special characters

- No number at the start

So, let's assign the name DeleteEmptyRows.

Shortcut key

Next you need to assign a shortcut to this macro. You can see that the dialog box shows Ctrl +. So, if you write any alphabet in the box, that alphabet along with the *Ctrl* key will be the shortcut for this macro. But keep in mind that almost every alphabet is already assigned as a shortcut in MS Office. For example, if you use *Ctrl + C* as the shortcut to run a macro, this will replace the default shortcut in MS Office; in other words, in future if you press *Ctrl + C* to copy any content (which is usually the case) but instead of copying, Excel will run the macro to which you assigned this shortcut. So, now the question arises how do we assign a shortcut key? Answer is, instead of just pressing an alphabet on your keyboard, press the *Shift* key and the *alphabet*. For example, if you want to use the alphabet *D*, press *Shift + D* and the shortcut for this macro will be *Ctrl + Shift + D*.

> **Note: It is not mandatory to always assign a shortcut key to a macro. You can leave this field blank and if you want to run a macro, you can use "*Alt + F8*" to view the list of all the macros you have created.**

Where to store a macro

As discussed earlier, whenever you record a macro, only your actions will get recorded, and in the backstage of Excel, these actions will be saved as different statements. So, whenever you run the macro, Excel executes these statements one by one so fast that the entire task is completed in just a few minutes or seconds). So when you ask Excel to store a macro, Excel actually stores those statements.

The drop-down menu of Store macro in will show the following three options:

- **This Workbook**: This will save the macro in the current workbook (that is, the coding of the macro will be saved in the current workbook). Further, you will need to save the workbook as a Macro Enabled Workbook.

- **New Workbook**: Choosing this option will open a new workbook and all the recorded statements will be saved in that workbook. Again you will need to save this workbook as Macro Enabled Workbook.

- **Personal Macro Workbook**: The only purpose of this workbook is to store macros. Also, by default this workbook is hidden (you can unhide it by using the Unhide command under the View tab).

Remember that anytime you want to run a macro the respective workbook should be open at the time. Specifically, if you choose to store the macro in This Workbook or New Workbook, then these should be open so that you can use the macro anywhere in your Excel program but this is not the case with Personal Macro Workbook because it is always open (even if it is hidden).

Description

You can enter a description of the macro as shown in the following *Figure 8.4*. This is optional:

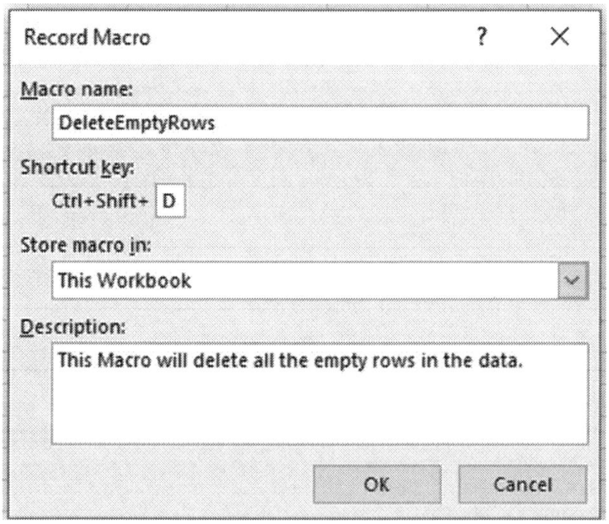

Figure 8.4

Click Ok.

Now recording is on.

To delete all the blank rows, first select a complete column, that is, starting from the column header | then go to Home tab and choose Find & Select. Go to Special, select Blanks, and then click Ok. Then right-click on any one of the selected blank cells, select Delete, and then select Entire row. Now stop the recording by clicking on the same place where you started recording.

Now your macro is recorded.

Save a Macro

Once you have recorded a macro, it's time to save it so that it is available for use in future. To do so, you need to first understand the file extension. The default file extension is .xlsx. However, this extension does not support macros; in other words, if you continue to work with this file extension, your macros will not be saved. So, you need to choose a macro-supporting file extension, that is, .xlsm. To save your workbook in this file format, go to the File tab, select Save As, and then choose this file extension. Or you can simply save the workbook by clicking on the Save button or by using keyboard shortcut *Ctrl + S*. This will immediately pop up an information dialog box. Here click No, go to Save As and save it in a macro-enabled file type (if you click Yes, Excel will save this workbook as a macro-free file. See the following *Figure 8.5*:

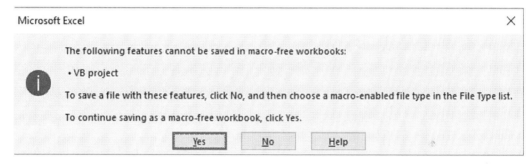

Figure 8.5

Run a Macro

To run a macro, make sure that the Excel file containing the macro is open. In our example, we have stored the macros in This Workbook, and so it must be open. Go to View tab, select the Macros group, and then select View Macros, or go to the Developer tab and select Macros. This will show a list of all the available macros. See the following *Figure 8.6*:

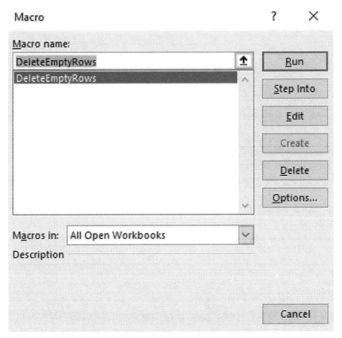

Figure 8.6

As there is only one macro in the list, to run it, you can either just click on it or click on **Run** or you can double-click on the name of the macro.

Assign Macro to an Object

You can assign a macro to almost any object (charts, shapes, pictures, smart art, etc.) that can be inserted in Excel. Let's insert a shape in our example and assign a macro to it. To perform this task, activate the sheet in which you want to insert the shape. Then go to **Insert** tab, select the **Illustrations** group, then **Shapes**, and finally **Rectangle: Rounded corners**. After drawing the shape on the sheet, you can insert some text in it, for example, Delete Empty Rows. Then right-click on the shape and select **Assign Macro**. This will open the same list of available macros. Double-click on the macro name to assign it to the shape. See the following *Figure 8.7*:

	D	E	F	G	H	I	J	K	L
e	Segment	Country	City	State	Postal Code				
	Consumer	United States	Henderson	Kentucky	42420				
	Consumer	United States	Henderson	Kentucky	42420				
f	Corporate	United States	Los Angeles	California	90036				
	Consumer	United States	Fort Lauderdale	Florida	33311		Delete Empty Rows		
	Consumer	United States	Fort Lauderdale	Florida	33311				
in	Consumer	United States	Los Angeles	California	90032				
in	Consumer	United States	Los Angeles	California	90032				
in	Consumer	United States	Los Angeles	California	90032				
in	Consumer	United States	Los Angeles	California	90032				

Figure 8.7

As the macro is assigned to this shape, it will act like a button, that is, a clickable shape. Clicking on this button will trigger your recorded macro, that is, Delete Empty Rows.

Check the VBA Code

As discussed earlier, our actions during macro recording get converted into statements and are saved at the backstage of Excel. So, let's just take a look at those statements for the macro we recorded above. To do so, go to the Developer tab, and select Visual Basic. This will open up VBE where you can see the VBA code (statements). If you see a completely grey window, then it's time to turn on Project Explorer, that is, a side pane that contains the list of all open workbooks, add-ins. Now go to the View tab and select Project Explorer. See the following *Figure 8.8*:

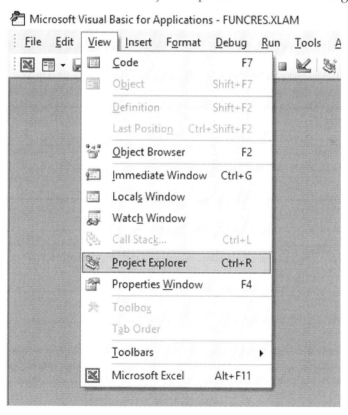

Figure 8.8

Now, you can see the Project Explorer window. As the Excel workbook in which we recorded the macro is open, we can expand the menu to reach Modules. Under this, you must see Module1. Just double-click on it and the Code Window will open on the right. See the following *Figure 8.9*:

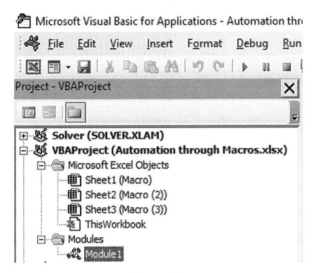

Figure 8.9

The code shown in *Figure 8.10* is the one that got recorded for our actions:

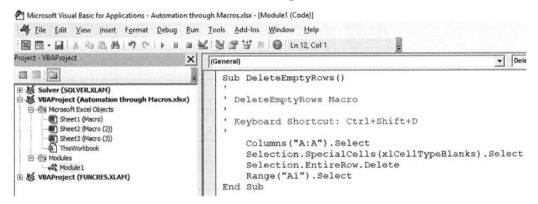

Figure 8.10

This code is actually not very difficult to understand even for a person without any programming background. As you can see, it starts with Sub, then the name of the macro, and ends with End Sub. Any statement starting with a single quote is a comment, and it won't be used during the process as it's just an information statements. In fact, you can turn any working statement into a comment by adding a single quote before it. Rest of the statements are straight forward as we can sense it out that I have selected the complete column A then went for the selection of special cells, that is, blanks then deleted the entire rows which were in selection and finally activated cell A1.

Edit or delete a Macro

Let's learn how to edit or delete a macro. To do so, you just need to select the list of available macros. You can go to the View tab, select the Macros group and then View Macros, or go to the Developer tab and select Macros. This will open a dialog box with a few options on the right. To delete or edit any macro, select it from the list. Deleting will remove the entire macro, that is, all its statements from the backstage; on the other hand, editing can be done on two levels, that is, either editing the code, or editing the shortcut or description. For this, you need to click on Macro Options. See the following *Figure 8.11*:

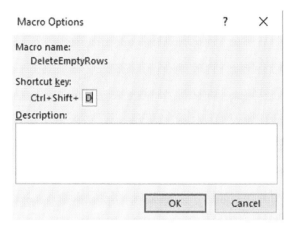

Figure 8.11

Macro security settings

In the world of programming, there are good and bad macros. Good macros can save a lot of your time, whereas bad macros can harm you, e.g., by removing files from your system or even injecting malware. For this reason, Microsoft has introduced macro-security features that you can turn on and protect your system every time you get a macro-enabled file. There are four security settings. To see the list, go to the Developer tab and select Security Settings. This will pop up a Trust Centre dialog box. See the following *Figure 8.12*:

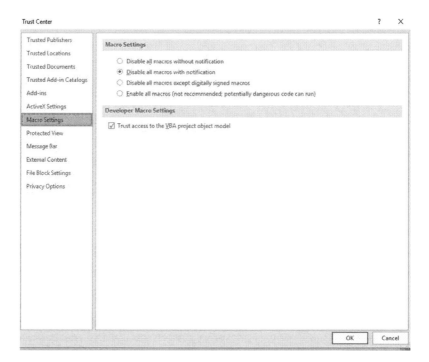

Figure 8.12

Let's understand the following four options:

- **Disable all macros without notification:** With this option, whenever you get a macro-enabled file and try to open the same, Excel will keep the macros disabled and won't even let us know about it.

- **Disable all macros with notification:** With this option, whenever you open a macro-enabled file, a security warning will appear above the formula bar asking you to click **Enable** only if you trust the source; else you can keep it disabled.

- **Disable all macros except digitally signed macros:** With this option, if you have already trusted the publisher of the digitally signed macro, then the macro will be enabled. Else you can notify Excel to trust the publisher in future, or you can keep it disabled.

- **Enable all macros (not recommended, potentially dangerous code can run):** This option will enable and run all macros. This could be dangerous as some malicious code could corrupt your system.

So, the best option is to always go with **Disable all macros with notification**, as we have control over it.

Summary

The purpose of this chapter was to give you an idea about macros and how to use them. Now you know how macros can save lot of effort and time.

The topic of Macros is vast, and although what we have covered here is just an introduction, you surely realize how amazing this tool is. You can learn more about VBA, by just considering different examples and data.

Index

Manufactured by Amazon.ca
Bolton, ON